Mad Stones: Their Use in Middle Tennessee, and Elsewhere.

By

CL Gammon

Deep Read Press

LAFAYETTE, TENNESSEE
deepreadpress@gmail.com

Copyright © 2025 by CL Gammon

All Rights Reserved.

The publisher prohibits reproduction, scanning, or distribution of this book in any printed or electronic form without written permission, except for brief passages quoted as part of a literary review.

Please do not take part in or encourage piracy of copyrighted materials in violation of the author's rights. Purchase only authorized editions.

The publisher does not control and does not assume any responsibility for the author's or any third-party websites or their content. Views expressed here are those of the author alone.

First Deep Read Press Edition.

Edited by: Kim Gammon

Cover Design by: Kim Gammon

Cover Photo by: Kim Gammon

ISBN: 978-1-954989-67-2

Published by:
DEEP READ PRESS
Lafayette, Tennessee
www.deepreadpress.com
deepreadpress@gmail.com

For Kim.

Other Local History Titles by CL Gammon

You can find all the local history titles listed below at Amazon or at the Deep Read Press website.

A Quarter Century of Macon County Crime (1960-1984)

Ballyhoo: John Butler and the Monkey Trial

Bizarre Murders in Tennessee: 13 True Stories

Blood on the Cumberland: The Battle of Hartsville

Chains and Dollars: The Slave Business in Middle Tennessee, Part 1

Death on the Highland: Spanish Flu in Macon County

Dixie Witches: 9 True Southern Witch Trials

Hanging the Macon County Witch

Highland Rim Warriors: Macon County Tennessee and World War II

Murder, Mayhem, and Moonshine: True Macon County Crime Stories

Revenue Raiders: Macon County's Whiskey War

Shallow Graves and Shattered Dreams: Solving the Murders of Three Macon County Men

The Fountain of Youth at Red Boiling Springs, Tennessee, Part 1

The Fountain of Youth at Red Boiling Springs, Tennessee, Part 2

The Macon County Race War

Tiger Strong! Macon County Football, 2024

Acknowledgements

There are many people who helped push this book along, directly, indirectly, or both.

Randy East, Macon County, Tennessee, Historian pointed me toward a source.

Shelta McCarter Shrum gifted me a number of materials a couple of years ago that serve as a never-ending fountain of information.

My wife Kim, as always, helped out in many ways, directly and indirectly.

I'd also like to mention the late June Shrum. She didn't help with this book directly, but she helped me out with so many projects in the past that she deserves recognition.

The late Harold G. Blankenship, former Macon County Historian, deserves mention. I consult the material he gathered in almost every local history title I write.

The late Betty M. Scott also deserves to be singled out. She worked many long hours in her efforts to help preserve Macon County history. We are forever indebted to her.

I'll also add that any errors that may be between the covers of this book are mine, and mine alone.

Contents

Introduction	p. 7
1. 1871-1875	p. 11
2. 1876-1880	p. 17
3. 1881-1885	p. 20
4. 1886-1890	p. 30
5. 1891-1895	p. 58
6. 1896-1900	p. 66
7. 1901-1905	p. 77
8. 1906-1910	p. 93
9. After 1910	p. 107
10. Cures and Preventatives	p. 110
11. Ancient Mad Stones	p. 116
About the Author	p. 118
Index	p. 119

Introduction

Hydrophobia was a death sentence until 1885, when a vaccine for it was developed. The vaccine became available in the United States the following year. Yet, even after the vaccine was developed and adopted for use, it was years before it was widely available.

In their desperation, as anyone would, those that had contracted rabies, or feared that they had, clutched at almost anything that would give them hope from the dread disease.

One "remedy" that was employed for many decades was called the "Mad Stone." Depending upon the person who possessed one, the Mad Stone was either "a vegetable substance or stone" which was formed in the digestive tracts (or elsewhere) of wild animals such as deer.

When pressed against a bite wound, the Mad Stone would stick to it and supposedly draw the rabies "venom" out. After a time, the Mad Stone would no longer stick to the area of the bite, which signaled that the venom was gone and that the victim was cured.

Even after proof was provided that Mad Stones failed to cure victims, people continued to seek out those with the magical stone in their vain hope of a cure. Again, this was natural. They simply had no alternative, so they had nothing to lose.

There were accepted "medical" treatments before the vaccine became available. One treatment involved amputating the digit or limb where the bite occurred. Another was to cauterize the wound. There was another treatment that involved "digging out" the bitten area. Still another treatment was "sucking out" the poison before it spread. None of those methods were effective in preventing symptoms from developing, or in preventing victims from dying from rabies.

Naturally, those fearing they had been exposed to rabies were, in their desperate hope to avoid the agony and death brought on by hydrophobia, quick to declare themselves cured after being treated by a Mad Stone. Over the decades in which its use was common, hundreds of relieved people claimed to be cured by the use of the rare Mad Stone.

Why did people claim to be cured by the magical treatment? There are two answers.

Firstly, extremely few of those who feared exposure had actually been bitten by rabid animals. In those cases, since there was no rabies present, it never manifested itself in them.

Secondly, while symptoms are sometimes present in a few days, it usually takes 30 to 50 days for them to appear. And in some cases, victims can appear to be healthy for a year or more before hydrophobia symptoms present themselves. Of course, if the hopeful patient appeared to be rabies free after a few days, he would almost certainly declare himself "cured."

Sadly, like all such pseudoscientific remedies, the Mad Stone did nothing but fill victims with false hope until the inevitable happened.

This small volume looks at the use of Mad Stones in Middle Tennessee and, to a lesser degree, elsewhere for the half century between 1871 and the early 1920s. Every case mentioned is documented by at least one source. Of course, documentation doesn't prove that the statements were accurate, and most of the "cured," patients were never infected in the first place.

The reader should keep in mind that this work only highlights the use of Mad Stones. There were many, many instances of Mad Stone use in Middle Tennessee and elsewhere that are not included here. There weren't more cases in Middle Tennessee than elsewhere, Middle Tennessee simply was simply the focus of the book.

There were hundreds of stories touting the benefits of Mad Stones. Additionally, there were many doctors that used them in their practices.

However, despite the anecdotal evidence, and their use by medical professionals, no true scientific evidence supporting Mad Stone use was ever produced.

Scientific evidence or not, many people, educated and uneducated alike, believed in the powers of Mad Stones and made use of the. Even famous and highly respected Americans used them. For instance, Abraham Lincoln even had one applied to his son, Robert Todd.

About this volume:

Spellings of names and locations were often haphazard in publications in bygone years. The author has taken pains to be as accurate as possible, but he was at the mercy of the documents he had to use, and he cannot guarantee that all the names and places listed here are completely accurate.

Dates listed here are presented as accurately as possible, but they may sometimes be estimates because exact dates are not available.

Each example begins with the state or the states with which it originates and the date (sometimes approximated) that the example occurred.

This volume includes a look at some of the statements made in support of Mad Stones and some of those made by opponents.

It also be noted that in older times, the term "rabies" applied only to animals, while "hydrophobia" applied only to humans. However, in more recent times the terms have been used interchangeably, and the author has followed the more recent convention.

Oddly, while some of those opposed to Mads Stone use attempted to provide scientific evidence to make their point, most relied on the same kind of anecdotal evidence that they scoffed at when produced by believers. Moreover, the attackers sometimes seemed to confirm that Mad Stones drew away the rabies virus from wounds.

Those fearful of having hydrophobia shouldn't be judged too harshly for using it before the Pasteur treatment was available. After all, what choice did they have? Hydrophobia is one of the most painful ways to die. One can hardly blame anyone for trying to avoid it, even if it meant turning to a magical stone from a deer's gut.

1. 1871-1875

1871

[Tennessee] February 7, 1871. A man who lived near Stones River came to Nashville in search of help for his young daughter. He said the girl had been bitten by a mad dog and he wanted someone to telegraph Lynchburg, Virginia where a man reputedly had a Mad Stone. He wanted the telegram to ask the man to bring the Mad Stone to Tennessee and treat the lass.

Much to the worried father's relief, he was told that there was no need to send to Virginia for a Mad Stone. There was a man named Alexander Joseph, a native New Yorker, who lived on Russell Street in the Edgefield district. Joseph, so the man was told, possessed a Mad Stone.

Happy with his good fortune, the relieved man carried his daughter to Edgefield, and Joseph treated her.

[Tennessee] May 24, 1871. A mad dog terrorized an area of Giles County about nine miles from Pulaski. The dog began its rampage outside the home of a woman named Hall. While there, it bit two of her children.

The dog then walked along Haywood Creek, biting everything in its path. It came upon a house where an African American family lived and bit two more children.

From there the sick animal proceeded along Richland Creek to the property owned by Robert Rodes and came upon a house that Rodes rented to a family. There it bit another child,

The rampage continued at the B. F. Carter farm where the mad dog bit several other canines. Finally, the dog went back to the Rodes farm where it was killed.

The Hall children, and the child living on the Rodes farm were treated with a Mad Stone and reportedly, "all the poison was drawn out and the children were safe and sound." The word was that the African American children were not given the benefit of the Mad Stone and they developed hydrophobia.

It was said that there were several Mad Stones in the area, and at least one person was advertising "Mad Stones for Sale" in the *Giles County Press*. The ad touted the Mad Stone's "wonderful efficacy as a preventative agent."

The crassness of marketing of Mad Stones for profit outraged prominent Giles County physician, Charles Clayton Abernathy. Abernathy attempted to expose and dispel the Mad Stone myth.

The doctor tried to impress upon the citizenry of Giles County how ridiculous relying upon Mad Stones to prevent hydrophobia was. He stated bluntly, "There is no cure for hydrophobia, and only one preventative, excision of the entire wound inflicted by the rabid animal." That is, the complete surgical amputation of the wound area. He continued that after being bitten, time was of the essence. The operation had to be conducted before virus from entered the bloodstream.

Dr. Abernathy also attempted to explode the myth that only dogs could transmit rabies. He pointed out that "all animals capable of inflicting a wound with the teeth" could transmit rabies to humans. He added that rabies was transmitted by saliva entering the blood stream through bites, or by coming into contact with open wounds.

The good doctor cautioned parents not to allow their children to play with dogs and cats until the rabies epidemic that gripped Giles County abated.

Abernathy finished by stating that he didn't want to "wound the feelings" of those that had believed in the virtues of Mad Stones. He merely wanted to warn the public that the superstition was of no value.

While Dr. Abernathy was quoting what was considered the best medical practice for rabies at the time, he was incorrect in a couple of notable ways. First, surgically removing wounded digits or limbs won't prevent the rabies. Once the rabid animal's saliva enters the body, removing the wounded area won't prevent the spread of the virus.

Secondly, the virus that causes rabies doesn't usually enter the bloodstream to spread. It commonly enters through nerve endings travels up the nerves to the spinal cord and brain.

[Tennessee] November 26, 1871. L. C. Johnson, who lived seven miles of Shelbyville, reported that his little daughter had been bitten by a mad dog a few days before. Johnson had scoured the surrounding counties before coming to Nashville in search of the magical Mad Stone that he hoped would save his child.

1872

[Kentucky] February 13, 1872. Jewett Butterfield, a police officer from the Louisville suburb of Portland, was took a bite from a "strange" greyhound. The dog showed no indication of being rabid, and Butterfield forgot the incident quickly.

Then, on April 9, Butterfield suddenly felt pain in in his arm "as if punctured by a thousand needles." The arm pain was followed by chills, and then convulsions. At first, the convulsions were 15 to 30 minutes apart, then they grew closer together.

Butterfield had a Mad Stone applied, but it had no effect. He suffered greatly before dying on April 18.

[Tennessee] April 10, 1872. While there were those that swore with faith their belief that the Mad Stone was a miracle cure, others scoffed at it and characterized it as a "silly superstition." One person wrote that the only way to get a Mad Stone to work would be to "throw it with great force at the dog before the bite is received."

1873

[Tennessee] September 18, 1873. Word was that there had been several mad dogs spotted in Henry County. All the dogs were killed, but not before "a young man was severely bitten by one of them." The story was that "the young man was carried to a Mad Stone, which was thoroughly applied."

Scoffing at the Mad Stone treatment, one newspaper reporter wrote, "We think it likely that a few *fool-stones* are needed in old Henry."

1874

[Tennessee] March 28, 1874. The son of William Owen who lived in Henry County was bitten by a dog that was feared to be rabid. A Mad Stone was applied and Owen felt his son was no longer in danger.

There was plenty of skepticism about the prophylactic quality of Mad Stones. One reason for that was the fact that it could take up to a year, or even longer, for symptoms to develop, and some of those declaring themselves cured developed rabies months later. When that happened, the reputation of the Mad Stone use on the bite victim wasn't damaged.

However, since there were few good options for those infected with the rabies virus, many physicians were unwilling to ignore any partial remedy.

[Tennessee] April 5, 1874. An epidemic of mad dogs had apparently broken out in West Tennessee and some of the good folk in that section of the state were searching frantically for a Mad Stone. In Nashville, the West Tennesseans were mocked for their "superstitions."

For the second time in about a year, there was a general slaughtering of dogs in Weakley County. However, it didn't curb the rabies problem there.

Near Dresden, John Bragg's child was bitten by a small dog owned by the family. Fearing the family pet might be rabid, Bragg took the child to a man with a Mad Stone. The man, James Baugh Dinwiddie, lived near Henry Station in Henry County. He was more than willing to use his Mad Stone to try to help the child.

Dinwiddie said his Mad Stone came from a much larger stone that had been in his family for generations. Dinwiddie continued that his father, Moses Dinwiddie, had broken the big Mad Stone into a dozen equal pieces and had given a piece to each of his 12 children.

[Tennessee] November 30, 1874. James Johnson was around nine-years-old. He lived at Flat Creek near Shelbyville with his brother. A mad dog bit him, and his brother took him to a man who applied a Mad Stone.

The wound healed, and James appeared to be cured. However, he developed the symptoms of hydrophobia on December 18, and after 24-hours of extreme agony, James died.

Chapter Sources:

"Bitten by a Mad Dog." *The Republican Banner*, November 26, 1871.

"Bitten by Mad Dog." *The Republican Banner*, April 4, 1874.

"By the Way." *The Republican Banner*, April 5, 1874.

"Death from Hydrophobia." *The Republican Banner*, December 27, 1874.

"Dreadful Case of Hydrophopia." *The Republican Banner*, April 19, 1872.

"Editorial Article." *The Republican Banner*, September 18, 1873.

"Five Children Bitten by a Mad Dog." *The Republican Banner*, June 3, 1871.

"Mad Dogs and Mad Stones." *The Republican Banner*, April 5, 1874.

"Mad Stone: A Popular Superstition Scientifically Exploded." *The Republican Banner*, June 18, 1871.

"Mad Stone." *The Republican Banner*, February 8, 1871.

"The Benefits of Walking." *The Republican Banner*, April 10, 1872.

2. 1876-1880

1876

[Iowa] July 1, 1876. Captain D. J. Bunce of Mechanicsville, Cedar County, Iowa, was bitten on the wrist by a small dog. At first, he didn't at first think it was rabid, but he killed it immediately, anyway.

Bunce didn't think much of the incident until July 4. On that day, he felt a sharp pain at the wound site. The pain extended to the back of his neck, and then around to his face. He said, "This would last but a moment, but it would return at intervals, each time getting worse."

Convincing himself that he was in serious danger of coming down with hydrophobia, Bunce began trying to learn where the nearest Mad Stone might be. On July 5, he was told that that a man named Turner Evans of Iowa City had one.

At 11 p.m. on July 5, a worried Bunce left on the 30-mile trip to Iowa City. However, the Cedar River was flooded, and that delayed his arrival until about noon on July 6.

Upon arriving in the city, Bunce learned that Evans had moved to the town of Paris in Linn County. Bunce made the 50 odd mile trip north to Paris, where he found Evans and learned that Evans shared joint ownership of the Mad Stone with a man named Fleming.

Evans applied the Mad Stone to Bunce's wound at about 5 p.m. on July 8. The Mad Stone stuck which convinced Bunce that "the dog which bit me was mad, and my system was becoming impregnated with the virus."

Bunce related that the Mad Stone "held on" for 25 minutes the first time it was applied. When it was full, it changed color and fell off. Bunce said the first treatment was very painful, but the pain reduced with each application.

Bunce continued that next, "Another scarification was made and it was again applied." The procedure was repeated 73 times! And on each of those 73 applications the Mad Stone stayed on for between 25 minutes and an hour. Finally, after the treatments that had gone on for between 30 hours and three days, the stone wouldn't adhere any more, and its color changed from a "dark brown" to a "deep green."

Evans and Fleming claimed to have saved many people in the past 25 years. Hundreds, the two said, attested to the powers of the Mad Stone.

Unlike most Mad Stone owners, Evans and Fleming also treated livestock with their Mad Stone. They said they had saved farmers in Paris thousands of dollars by preventing cattle from getting hydrophobia.

[Tennessee] July 27, 1876. A. Dooley who lived on McGavock Street in Nashville, said she could cure hydrophobia "in man or beast, in nine days." Witnesses to her technique, said Dooley had never failed to cure those afflicted with rabies. Dooley didn't reveal what her technique was, but the assumption was that it involved a Mad Stone.

1877

[Arizona and Texas] December 22, 1877. Several years earlier while in Arizona, a Texan had killed a deer, and he had taken a Mad Stone from it. He had applied the Mad Stone to bite wounds several times and, according to him, it had never failed to "extract the poison of mad dogs, snakes, tarantulas, and other venomous creatures."

A druggist in Waco wanted the Mad Stone so badly that he paid the owner $250 for it.

1880

[Tennessee and Pennsylvania] May 14, 1880. W. S. Cloyd of Green Hills community of Davidson County requested information as to where in Tennessee he could find a Mad Stone. He wanted to locate the nearest one to Nashville, and the name of the man that had it.

On May 20, Joseph Barbiere of Philadelphia responded to Cloyd. He said that he believed there were only three real Mad Stones in all of the United States. He continued that he had seen one of them. A Mr. Fitzwilson owned it. Mr. Fitzwilson, so said Barbiere, was an agent of the Fidelity Mutual Aid Society, and he lived at 908 Chestnut Street, Philadelphia, Pennsylvania.

Barbiere described the Mad Stone as being black or of deep brown color, and he said it was "about the size of a small block of India ink." That is, the Mad Stone was about two inches long by an inch and a half wide.

The descriptions of Mad Stones varied widely. For instance, in the West, they were sometimes described as about the size of an English walnut and somewhat porous. This volume relates several ways Mad Stones were described.

Chapter Sources:

"A Mad Dog's Bite." *The Republican Banner*, July 26, 1876.

"In Search of a Mad Stone." *The Daily American*, May 16, 1880.

"No Title." *The Daily American*, December 22, 1877.

"The Mad Stone." *The Daily American*, May 20, 1880.

3. 1881-1885

1881

[Missouri and Nebraska] January 25, 1881. There was a story of a man from Tecumseh, Nebraska who had been bitten by a rabid pig. Fearing the horrors of rabies, the man traveled all the way to Savannah, Missouri to get treatment from the "famous Mad Stone owned by Old John Nelson."

Nelson applied the Mad Stone on the Nebraskan's wound and it adhered to it "from early morn until sundown, when it dropped off." The satisfied patient departed "feeling that he had been cured."

Uncle Tom Nelson had owned his Mad Stone since 1848, and over the next 33 years he claimed to have "used it in over a hundred cases where men have been bitten" and, continued Nelson, "it never failed to work a cure."

1882

[Tennessee] January 9, 1882. Bud Hayes of the Bunker Hill community of Giles County came to Pulaski in search of treatment for a dog bite. Fearing the dog was rabid, Hayes stopped by the home of G. A. Hopkins and purchased a Mad Stone. It's uncertain what he paid for it, but some Mad Stones were allegedly sold for as much as $7,500.

After leaving the Hopkins home, Hayes visited the office of Dr. Charles Clayton Abernathy and received the accepted medical treatment for his wound.

A week after suffering the bite, Hayes was still experiencing no symptoms of rabies and he was certain he had been cured.

[New York and Pennsylvania] January 18, 1882. There had been a rash of hydrophobia deaths "real or imagined" in New York and Pennsylvania. The deaths seemed to disprove the myth that animals only became rabid in the warmer months, because some of the deaths took place in the wintertime. Evidently, Mad Stones had no effect above the Mason-Dixon Line.

Below are some of the recent deaths in New York and Pennsylvania attributed to rabies:

Frederick Kroger of New York, age 11, died June 8, 1881, from a bite received April 2, 1881.

James Kavanaugh of New York, age 12, died August 9, 1881, from a bite received on April 15, 1881.

Henry B. Comley of Philadelphia died on Christmas Day 1881 from a bite received in 1878. It was believed that his death was the result of "fear more than anything else."

Fred Miller of Philadelphia died on January 7, 1882. It was believed that his death was the result of "fear more than anything else."

John Baker of New York died on January 10, 1882, from a bite received in October 1881.

Welcome Arnold of Buffalo died on February 21, 1881, from a bite he received from a dog in 1873 who was believed to have hydrophobia. Arnold had his first seizure in 1877, and it was believed that he had recovered. Of all the cases listed above, the Arnold case is the least believable.

[Iowa] July 24, 1882. Authur Goodpasture of Waterloo, Iowa had earlier been bitten by a mad died. He contracted hydrophobia and died despite the fact that a Mad Stone had been applied to his wound.

[Mississippi] December 4, 1882. Ben Milan of Marshall County, Mississippi, owned a well-known Mad Stone. He claimed his "wonderful" Mad Stone had been applied in 1,229 cases. and everyone receiving treatment had survived. He said he treated about 15 people annually for mad dog bites.

Milan related that in 1810, a Dr. Baker from Alabama brought the Mad Stone from China where it was called the "snake-stone." In China, the snakestone was used to draw out the venom left by snake, spider, and insect bites. Soon after Baker returned to Alabama, he tested it on dog bites "with great success." He continued to use the stone until his death.

After Baker died, his Mad Stone was sold to a group four neighbors. One member of the group was Garvis Milan, Ben's father. The other three owners eventually sold their shares to the elder Milan.

Upon his death, Garvis Milan willed the Mad Stone to Ben. Within days of receiving it, Ben was offered the hefty sum of $7,500 for his Mad Stone. In those days, $7,500 amounted to more than 13 years of normal wages in Mississippi. Even though he had a king's ransom in front of him, Milan refused to sell his Mad Stone.

Milan's numbers are interesting. If his Mad Stone had treated 1,229 people, and if 15 people were treated annually, then the first treatment would have occurred in 1800, or a decade before it was brought to America.

1883

[Tennessee] June 18, 1883. Word from Smithville was that Walker Moore's young son would survive a dog bite. On June 11, the younger Moore was bitten by what was feared to be a rabid mongrel. Moore transported the boy to Coffee County where a Mad Stone was applied to the wound.

Moore explained the process. The Mad Stone was applied to the area of the wound and it adhered to it for one and one-quarter hours before it fell off. Then the stone was reattached until it fell off again. The Mad Stone was reattached several times more, and each time it for a shorter period before falling off again. Finally, it would not stick at all, and the boy was declared cured.

Monte Pirtle lived near Moore. His son was also bitten on June 11, but Pirtle didn't learn of it until five days later. As soon as he did learn of it, he took his son for Mad Stone treatment as well.

[Tennessee] July 23, 1883. In early July 1883, in Smithville, a little girl was bitten on the ankle by a rabid cat. The next day, her father carried her to Coffee County where a Mad Stone was applied to her wound. The father swore that "the poison had been extracted" and that she was cured.

The possessor of the Mad Stone said it was the third or fourth time he had used it on a bite victim, and that it had "proven satisfactory in every instance."

[Tennessee] September 9, 1883. A man named Greenville Fletcher, who lived in Coffee County, possessed the Mad Stone (not the one from Coffee County mentioned in the previous paragraphs). He said he had used it on 22 different bite victims and not one of them had developed hydrophobia.

Fletcher described his Mad Stone as black and smooth, about one and one-quarter inches long, three-quarters of an inch wide, and three-eighths of an inch thick.

Fletcher, who said he never charged for the use of the Mad Stone, explained that his marvelous mineral wouldn't attach to anything except bites that contained poison. Fletcher continued that once the Mad Stone took hold, it could not without tearing the flesh, be pulled loose until it had absorbed all the poison from the wound. Since it always took out all the poison on the first application, it could never be used on the same wound twice.

When the allegedly curative stone fell off the wound, Fletcher placed it into a pan warm water and it crackled like hot rock being submerged in frigid water. After being immersed for about five minutes, the Mad Stone would be ready for another use.

How did he get the Mad Stone? Fletcher explained that in 1876 or 1877 his son, who was operating a farm in Virginia, fell ill at about harvest time. Fletcher collected a group of men and they went with him to his son's farm and harvested the crop. As Fletcher returned home, he met a family on their way to Texas and they traveled together.

Upon arriving back in Coffee County, Fletcher opened his home to the Texas family so they could rest for a few days before continuing their long, arduous journey to the Lone Star State. The woman in the party had two Mad Stones and she repaid the kindness shown to her by giving Fletcher's wife one of them. She had, as Fletcher's story went, been offered $300 for the wonderful rock, but she had refused to part with it.

[Florida] October 30, 1883. A Pensacola, Florida man had a Mad Stone he said he took from a Deer's stomach in 1853. He had been applying it for 30 years with impressive results.

[Indiana and Illinois] December 17, 1883. A man named Elledge who lived near Paris, Illinois brought his nine-year-old son to Terre Haute, Indiana to have the famous "Terre Haute Mad Stone" applied.

The boy was displaying "many symptoms of hydrophobia." According to Elledge, the symptoms began about December 10. On that day, the child "refused to cross a small stream, and at the sight of the water ran around in a circle." A day or two later, the boy refused to drink water, and he refused to sit at a table if he could see a glass of water.

Since December 14, the boy was having five to ten spams a day. He crawled on his hands and knees, barking and growling like a dog, and "resisting physical control with miraculous strength." However, "a pat on the head and a command to lie still, as one would speak to a dog," would quiet him.

After the strange behavior began, the boy told Elledge that he had had been bitten by a dog on August 13. The boy then showed his a father a scar on his knee that was the result of the dog bite.

The famous Terre Haute Mad Stone was applied, apparently to the scar on the boy's knee. However, after two fruitless hours the Mad Stone still would not adhere or drawn away any rabies virus. At that point, the Mad Stone practitioner gave up on the effort. A despondent Elledge took his son home with little hope of his son's recovery.

For the record, none of the boy's symptoms were in any way those of a person with hydrophobia.

The Terre Haute Mad Stone had been well-known for decades. A credible story states that in 1852, Abraham Lincoln's nine-year-old son, Robert Todd, suffered a dog bite. Fearing hydrophobia, the future President took the boy from Springfield, Illinois, to Terre Haute. There, the celebrated Mad Stone was applied. The treatment was declared a success, as Robert Todd Lincoln never developed rabies.

1884

[Tennessee] July 23, 1884. Benjamin W. Franklin, who was about 10, lived with his family in the Fayette County community of La Grange. Benjamin was bitten by a mad dog, and the lad's father, Dr. William E. Franklin, sucked what he believed to be the poison out of the wound. After the procedure it appeared that the child had recovered.

Then in September the boy went into convulsions and displayed the symptoms of hydrophobia. Five doctors were called in, and a Mad Stone was brought in from Mississippi and applied, but nothing helped. After a terrible ordeal, the boy died.

Naturally, those that believed in the otherworldly powers of the Mad Stone claimed that it would have worked had it been applied earlier.

[Tennessee] October 1, 1884. Around midnight, Mack Fisher, a farmer living in Chattanooga, awoke to the sound of dogs fighting. Fisher, still in his nightclothes, hurried outside and saw a "ferocious" dog attacking his favorite English Setter.

Fisher tried to break up the fight, which caused the strange dog to turn on him. The dog sank its razor-sharp teeth into the man, causing deep wounds to Fisher's arm and thigh. Fisher could only get the dog to stop its attack by grabbing it by the hind legs and slamming it to the ground, killing it.

Early on October 2, the determination was that the strange dog was rabid. Fisher's friends then began to search for a Mad Stone to apply to Fisher's wounds. However, many of them believed that his death was "inevitable."

1885

[Tennessee] May 9, 1885. A mad dog bit two men, H. C. Gilmore and Robert Dies, in the Hunter's Point Community of Wilson County near the Trousdale County line. Gilmore was bitten on one finger, and Dies suffered wounds to the to his right cheek and upper lip.

The incident began when a man living in Trousdale County named Belcher had a big white dog go mad. The dog attacked a number of animals, including several dogs, before it was killed. One of the dogs bitten belonged to Dies, and Dies killed it immediately. However, another of the dogs bitten by Belcher's dog belonged to a man named King. For some reason that dog wasn't killed. King's dog bit several other dogs and it also bit Gilmore and Dies.

Gilmore immediately went to Lebanon and had a doctor amputate his finger. Due to the location of his wounds, amputation wasn't an option for Dies. He felt his best chance of survival was to use a Mad Stone, and he went in search of one.

Dies learned of Greenville Fletcher and his celebrated Mad Stone. However, before going to Coffee County, Dies first traveled the short distance to Macon County and visited Dr. Elijah Bratton in Lafayette.

Although he was one of the most respected medical men in Middle Tennessee, Bratton had a Mad Stone. The doctor applied the miracle stone to Dies' cheek. It stuck and appeared to work. However, it wouldn't stick to Dies' lip.

Dissatisfied with the treatment he received from Bratton, Dies continued on to Coffee County and paid Fletcher a visit. Fletcher applied his Mad Stone to the wounds and it stuck to both the cheek and the lip.

On May 14, Dies returned home. He happily stated that the Mad Stone had stayed attached for 20 hours, and it absorbed all the poison. He was certain that the wonderful Mad Stone had cured him. Sadly, shortly thereafter, it became apparent that Dies wasn't cured after all.

One day soon thereafter, while working in his fields, Dies became thirsty, and he walked to his house to get a drink of water. However, he found he couldn't swallow it.

Dies soon exhibited all the symptoms common with full-blown hydrophobia, including experiencing spasms, and tremendous pain. His agony grew so intense that he pleaded with family members to kill him. Of course, his relatives wouldn't murder him. Instead, they summoned doctors to aid the poor man.

For some time, Dies was thrashing about so much that no one could go into his room and assist him. Finally, family members were able to enter the room. They used ropes to secure Dies to a wall. Then, a doctor injected him with a large dosage of morphine. However, the pain was so great that the morphine had no effect on Dies.

The poor, tormented man tore his own flesh and beat his head against the wall until June 20, when his terrible ordeal ended in death.

[Tennessee] June 15, 1885. A mad dog bit J. A. Dunmon of Petersburg in Lincoln County. Dunmon traveled immediately to nearby Flintville, where he received a Mad Stone treatment from a Dr. Price. However, Dunmon wasn't certain that the treatment had been successful.

[Tennessee] June 23, 1885. A Mrs. Swanner who lived in Rutherford County was mauled by a mad dog. She received bite wounds on both her arms and on one of her breasts.

On June 26, Swanner traveled with a man called Mr. Potter to Coffee County so she could receive the Mad Stone treatment from the famous Greenville Fletcher.

Upon their return, Potter reported that there were several people from various parts of the state at Fletcher's house receiving the benefits of his well-known Mad Stone. From the statements Potter made, it was clear that rabies was rampant throughout the Midstate.

Chapter Sources:

"A Mississippi Man." *The Daily American*, November 17, 1882.

"A Stone with a History." *The Daily American*, December 4, 1882.

Blankenship, Harold G. *History of Macon County, Tennessee.* Tompkinsville, Kentucky: Monroe County Press, 1986.

"Chattanooga." *The Daily American*, October 3, 1884.

"Display Ad." *The Daily American*, January 25, 1881.

"How a Mad-Stone Failed." *The Daily American*, December 17, 1883.

"Live State News." *The Daily American*, June 19, 1885.

"Live State News." *The Daily American*, May 19, 1885.

Masters, Edgar Lee. *Lincoln the Man.* London: Cassell and Company, 1931.

"No Title." *The Daily American*, July 24, 1882.

"Over the State." *The Daily American*, January 16, 1882.

"Rabid Dogs on the Rampage." *The Daily American*, June 27, 1885.

Scott, Betty M. (Project Manager). *Macon County Tennessee, History and Families*. Paducah, Kentucky: Turner Publishing Company, 2001.

"The Cure of Hydrophobia." *The Daily American*, January 18, 1882.

"The Horrors of Hydrophobia." *The Daily American*, June 26, 1885.

"The Mad Stone." *The Daily American*, September 9, 1883.

"The South." *The Daily American*, October 30, 1883.

"The State at Large." *The Daily American*, July 23, 1884.

"The State at Large." *The Daily American*, June 18, 1883.

"The State at Large." *The Daily American*, September 23, 1883.

4. 1886-1890

1886

[New York] January 2, 1886. The American Pasteur Institute filed its certificate of incorporation in New York. The non-profit corporation's stated objective was: "The gratuitous care and treatment, by the Pasteur system of inoculation, of all persons threatened with or of suffering from hydrophobia."

While the Pasteur treatment had officially made it to the United States, it wouldn't be widely available in most locations for a considerable amount of time. Beyond that, for decades other treatments for hydrophobia, especially Mad Stones, remained more popular and better trusted than the Pasteur treatment.

[Tennessee] January 25, 1886. The citizens living in the southern parts of Moore County were gravely concerned about the considerable number of rabid dogs there. Mad dogs had reportedly bitten horses, cattle, hogs, sheep, geese, and other animals.

Shotgun sales in Moore County had increased greatly, and a number of dogs had been killed indiscriminately.

A dog bit Mark Bryant's little girl and he took her to a Mr. Shelton's house. There, Shelton applied a Mad Stone to her wound.

[Tennessee] January 25, 1886. The debate as to how to treat and prevent rabies raged for years. One man from Lynchburg, Tennessee claimed to have the solution. He said he had a cure and preventative for rabies that could be applied without killing mad dogs, or by applying Mad Stones. He promised to reveal his method if the United States government would first pay him $100,000. No one from Washington ever contacted him.

[Kentucky] March 5, 1886. A dog believed to be rabid bit Charles Reed of Simpson County. On March 12, Reed traveled to Bowling Green and was treated by a Mad Stone. The Mad Stone "stuck tightly to the bitten place, and his face looked like a ray of sunshine" when he returned home. Reed was happy that he had "averted a horrible death from hydrophobia by the use of the Mad Stone."

[Tennessee] June 12, 1886. Hardeman County resident Young Halloway was working on his farm when his own dog attacked him. Halloway feared the dog might have rabies and four days later, the farmer went to Bolivar in search of a Mad Stone.

A helpful citizen informed Halloway that a Miss Carraway had one of the "wonderful curiosities" which he sought. Carraway's Mad Stone had reputedly never failed "to afford relief."

The Halloway case caused a reporter from Bolivar to wonder why American scientists didn't acquire Mad Stones, analyze their properties, and learn what made them work. When the secret of their curative powers were discerned, the scientists could reproduce them artificially. After that, Mad Stones could be made available to all that needed them.

[Texas] August 8, 1886. A rabid dog bit little Walter Gandy, age 4. Walter lived on a farm near Fort Worth, Texas with his family. The dog's upper fangs entered the boy's face above eye. The canine's lower teeth punctured the flesh on Walter cheek.

The little boy didn't demonstrate any immediate symptoms of hydrophobia. Understandably, the only pain the boy complained of was his lacerated face.

Despite the lack of symptoms, the boy's father, W. K. Gandy, didn't want to gamble. He took Walter to north about 40 miles to Denton where a Mad Stone was applied. The Mad Stone would not adhere, and the Mad Stone applicator decided that no rabies virus was in Walter's system.

The elder Gandy wasn't satisfied with the result of the Mad Stone application. He took the boy from Denton about 55 miles south to Mansfield where another Mad Stone was available. That Mad Stone was applied as well, with the same result. Gandy brought the boy home hoping for the best, but uncertain what would happen.

On August 21, Walter complained of a sore throat and he was unable to eat anything. There were reports that he would cry when water was brought near him, and that he became extremely nervous. Several doctors were called in, but they couldn't help Walter.

Walter grew worse. "Greenish foam issued from his mouth," and his cries from his fierce pain were almost too much for his parents to endure.

On the morning of August 25, one of Walter's playmates paid him a visit. Walter snapped at the other boy, biting him slightly on the face. The doctors feared that Walter had infected the other boy with the rabies virus too.

During the evening of August 25, Walter grew quiet, then he dozed off to sleep, but only for a few moments. His parents said, "He awoke with a tremor, barked like a dog, bent himself double, gnashed his teeth, blood and foam gushed from his mouth, and he was dead."

[Tennessee and Texas] September 24, 1886. A "real" Mad Stone arrived in Nashville. The stone, which was credited with curing hundreds of people, was allegedly brought to North Carolina from England, and then around 1880, it was taken Texas. In Texas, a man named Bumpus lived at Farmersville, about 40 miles northeast of Dallas, gained possession of it.

Texans from miles around came to Farmersville and had their dog bites treated. But that wasn't all; Bumpus also used his Mad Stone to treat rattlesnake bites as well. Bumpus claimed that his Mad Stone was always effective.

Bumpus had a detailed and precise method of applying his Mad Stone and apparently, he never deviated one iota from his procedure. His method included the following steps:

1. Make an incision at the wound site the same size of the Mad Stone.
2. Soak the Mad Stone well in warm water.
3. Bind the Mad Stone to the place of the incision.
4. If there was no poison in the wound, the Mad Stone wouldn't adhere to it and the treatment stopped. But if there was poison present, the Mad Stone would "hold on like a leech until every bit" of the poison was absorbed.
5. When it released itself from the wound, the Mad Stone was placed in warm milk and the poison, greenish in color, would leave the stone and enter the milk. It was then ready to be applied to the next patient.

Bumpus sent the Mad Stone to his brother-in-law, a man named Rodney Wetherby. Wetherby passed it on a Dr. Hallowell of Nashville for the doctor's use.

Wetherby described the Mad Stone as being about one and one-half inches long, and three-quarters of an inch wide. Wetherby said he had witnessed the curative powers of the Mad Stone at work several times, and it had always completely cured those to whom it was applied. He mentioned on case in particular concerning three men had been bitten by a "very rabid dog." Two of the men had the Mad Stone applied and they never developed hydrophobia. The third man, according to Wetherby, took the "ordinary" treatment, and he soon became rabid and died.

[Mississippi] December 8, 1886. A mad dog bit Robert Hanks, a farmer from New Albany, Mississippi. Some of his concerned friends advised Hanks to have his wound treated by a Mad Stone. Hanks heeded his friends and he went to Waterford, and had a Mad Stone applied to his wound. The Mad Stone adhered for most of two days before falling off. After his "successful" treatment, Hanks returned home feeling safe from hydrophobia.

Hanks gave little more thought to the dog bite until the morning of February 17, 1887. He awakened with a "burning thirst," but when his wife handed water to him, "he went into violent convulsions." Hanks was in severe pain until the morning of February 22, when he died.

1887

[Georgia] March 15, 1887. Fear of hydrophobia gripped much of Georgia and threw many people into a state of hysteria. In a period of two weeks, several communities had been visited by a plague of rabid dogs. Groups of heavily armed Georgians scoured the counties of Banks, Hancock, Troupe, Elbert, and Forsythe. Every time the men came upon a dog, they opened fire upon it.

The paranoia in Georgia was immense, but the threat was also real. In Homer, Georgia the 10-year-old son of a Mr. Lockhart, died of rabies on March 13. The youngster suffered intense pain until he slipped into a coma from which he never awakened.

Troupe County was also in the clutches of mad dog mania. A dog belonging to a Dr. Roberts ran away and it was missing for several days before returning on March 12. When it did come home it appeared to have hydrophobia. The dog bit an 80-year-old man named Borders. Within three days, Mr. Borders went into convulsions.

The rampaging dog bit five other people, all of them women or children, and as many as 100 head of livestock. The number people the dog bit necessitated that Mad Stones be "sent for in all directions."

Mrs. Wash Lynn was "terribly lacerated" by a mad dog near Sparta, Georgia.

More than 50 mad dogs were believed to be running wild in Cherokee County, Georgia. A vicious canine bit three children of a Mr. Eleck were bitten. Additionally, a "strange disease" believed to be hydrophobia, infected the cattle there.

In Canton, Georgia a young cow broke loose while grazing. It then ran all over town "clearing the streets and knocking down fences." The cow then stomped off into the woods and "died in great agony."

State authorities were trying to determine the cause of the epidemic, but they had no real clues.

[Tennessee] April 17.1887. Even though the rabies vaccine was becoming more available throughout the United States, the Mad Stone was as popular as ever.

Watt G. Clark, who lived near the town of Eagleville in Rutherford County, let it be known that he had acquired a Mad Stone. He said it came from Florida, and it had been tested on numerous occasions in dog bite cases. Clark promised that it had proven to be "quite effective."

Considering that there always seemed to be an abundance of mad dogs loose in Rutherford County, Clark believed that his Mad Stone would be quite useful there.

1888

[Tennessee] February 12, 1888. Willow Green lived on the Lynchburg and Shelbyville Road near the Coffee County-Franklin County lines. Green's 12-year-old son was bitten on the right hand by what was believed to be a rabid dog.

Green wasted no time before taking the boy to Flintville in Lincoln County to the home of a Mr. Sheppard. First, Sheppard applied a Mad Stone to a bruise on the boy's hand where the dog's teeth didn't break the skin. The Mad Stone didn't stick to the bruise.

Then, Sheppard placed the Mad Stone on the wound where the dog's teeth had penetrated the skin. This time, the Mad Stone "stuck so tightly that it could not be pulled away without tearing the flesh from the hand." The stone remained affixed to the lad's hand for about 20 minutes, then it dropped off. Sheppard then took the "charged" Mad Stone and boiled it in salt water and milk to drain it of the poison it had absorbed.

After the Mad Stone had been cleansed of the rabies virus, Sheppard reattached it to the boy's wound and it stuck for another 15 or 20 minutes.

After the Milk Stone was cleaned again, Sheppard tried to stick it to the wound for a third time, but it wouldn't adhere again. With that, Green took his son home happy in the belief that the boy had been cured and that the lad wouldn't have to face the horrors of hydrophobia.

Sheppard fed some of the water and milk he had boiled the Mad Stone in to a chicken and it died within 15 minutes.

As for the mad dog, it was killed and left to rot. "Buzzards" ate the decaying carcass, and apparently many of the scavenger birds died from the contaminated dog flesh.

Sheppard said he got his Mad Stone from an "old" Baptist preacher who had extracted it from a red deer. The preacher had made Sheppard promise to never accept any compensation for treating people with his Mad Stone.

One of the myths about Mad Stones were that they were taken from only white deer. As seen from the above, sometimes people took them from deer that were other colors.

[Tennessee] February 12, 1888. Penny Ann Sullenger, age 62, who lived at Smithland in Lincoln County, was bitten on the arm by a mad dog. A Mad Stone was quickly placed on her wound and it stuck to it. The wound healed, she had no symptoms, and all appeared to be fine with her.

Then on July 4, Sullenger began to experience "violent pains in the wounded arm" which ran to her neck. She became thirsty, but she couldn't swallow. Sullenger suffered in agony until July 7, when she died.

[Tennessee] March 10, 1888. John Henry lived near the Big Harpeth River in Williamson County. Reports were that his dog had gone mad and had rampaged through the area. First, the dog entered the home of a man named Moran. While Moran's little girl was petting the dog, a goose walked past the open door. The canine spotted the goose, jumped on it, and tore it to shreds.

The dog roamed across an expanse of 11 miles and then it was finally killed. Before it was subdued, the rabid brute bit numerous dogs, cattle, horses, and hogs. Two of the hogs belonging to James Brown developed rabies and he had to kill them.

While the dog was blowing through the area like a whirlwind, it bit two boys who tried to play with it. The boys, Murray Greer and Mose Vaughn, were taken to a Mad Stone practitioner, who applied the stone to their wounds four times each.

Terrified that rabies would overwhelm the area, virtually all the dogs that came into contact with Henry's animal were killed, and all the farm animals were penned up until it was certain that they were free of rabies.

[Tennessee] July 22, 1888. A young man, named Forrest Wheeler lived on the corner of Monroe and Clay Streets in Nashville. He was bitten by a dog he feared might be rabid. The dog, a family pet, was acting very peculiarly, and Wheeler decided to put it in the cellar to see if it developed hydrophobia. When he picked up the dog, it bit Wheeler on the right hand. The dog was subsequently killed, and Wheeler went on the search for a Mad Stone practitioner.

Wheeler's injuries couldn't have been avoided by legislation, but a widespread outbreak of rabies might have been. In order to stem chances of a rabies epidemic in Nashville, the city government passed an ordinance in early July mandating that all dogs be muzzled when in public, otherwise they would be subject to being impounded. The dog muzzling ordinance was largely ignored, and the police found that enforcing it was impossible.

About 8:30 p.m. on July 23, a mad dog was spotted on the corner of Foster and First Streets. The dog was killed by a police officer named Vining, but not before it had bitten several other mongrels, some of which got away. There had been several people on the street, but none of them were bitten.

While concern hadn't risen to the level of general hysteria, a number of Nashvillians were afraid that a pack of mad dogs might be lurking around the next corner. Word was that almost everyone on the streets had an umbrella handy to ward off beastly canines, rabid or not. Moreover, the police were redoubling their efforts to impound unmuzzled dogs. They often shot the dogs they couldn't capture.

Still, citizens didn't think the streets were safe. Another young man was bitten on June 24, and six mad dogs were reported spotted in the Edgefield district of town.

Also, on the afternoon of June 24, Captain C. H. Bader shot a mad dog on the corner of Cheatam Street and Buena Vista Pike. The dog had allegedly been terrorizing the area for several hours.

[Tennessee] July 25, 1888. The fear of a massive rabies epidemic in Nashville continued to grow and local media sought to reel in the rising paranoia. A lengthy article related what rabies was thought to be, what the dangers really were, and how to treat wounds caused by suspected bites from rabid animals.

The article stated that the rabies threat was more imagination than reality. It was expressed that even if bitten by a rabid animal, the odds of a human developing hydrophobia was only about one in six.

Even today, most people won't believe it, but the odds stated in the article were remarkably close to being accurate. Today, we know, depending upon the rabid animal, the location of the bite, and the amount of virus transmitted, there is only about a 15% chance of contracting rabies. Of course, if one is bitten, he should get immediate treatment.

The article's author also understood that the rabies virus was transmitted through salvia, and it had to enter the system in order to cause hydrophobia. Merely getting salvia on the skin wasn't enough to cause hydrophobia.

Heavy clothing could inhibit the transmission of rabies. Garments could keep the animal's teeth from breaking the skin. The article also made the dubious statement that even if the animal's teeth did pass through one's clothing and break the skin, rabies would be prevented. The idea was that the cloth "cleans the tooth as it passes through" and no salvia would enter the wound.

The article stated that the greatest risk was in mistaking a rabid beast from a healthy one. It was pointed out that the image of a mad dog rushing through towns "growling at and chawing everything in his way" was largely a myth. The truly dangerous animal was characterized as "the dusty, dilapidated sleepy dog with his head and tail hung down and ropy salvia issuing from his mouth."

Another myth the article exploded was that mad dogs had "a horror of water." The article pointed out that in truth rabid dogs have trouble swallowing, but they have no fear of water.

Still another myth exposed was actually based on fact. It was known that the rabies virus usually found its way to the spine. From that fact a myth arose that since a dog's tail was part of its spine, if the end of a dog's tail were chopped off, it could never contract rabies.

But what people most wanted to know was what they should do if they were bitten. The article presented the accepted medical remedies. The person bitten was encouraged to "cut around in the healthy flesh and remove the bruised part and cauterize the fresh surface." Or more simply, cut out the wound and cauterize the place where the bite marks had been.

Another treatment mentioned was to "open the wound deeper so as to allow it to bleed freely and wash out the salvia or apply a suction apparatus and draw the salvia from the wound."

Then there was the Mad Stone for those "not inclined to be skeptical."

The article described the Mad Stone as "black, susceptible of a high polish, and has the texture of slate." The article repeated the common idea that when applied the Mad Stone adhered to the wound, it absorbed the poison, and then when all the poison was absorbed, it dropped off the wound. To be cleaned, the mad stone had to be thrown fresh milk.

The article compared the Mad Stone's action to the "celebrated snake stone of India." But the Mad Stone differed from the India stone in that it was black, and the Indian stone was blue.

[Tennessee] July 25, 1888. It was pointed out publicly again that Alexander Joseph of the Edgefield district had a Mad Stone that had cured several people and that he would treat anyone who needed his help.

[Tennessee] November 23, 1888. Sam Whitworth, who lived near Fairfield in Bedford County, let it be known that he had a Mad Stone and that he was willing to apply it to anyone who needed treatment for rabies.

1889

[Tennessee] February 11, 1889. F. R. Holden of Iron City, Wayne County, arrived in Columbia, Tennessee with seven-year-old Oscar Wiggington.

Little Oscar had been bitten by a dog about 10 miles from Iron City on February 2. The little boy had gone to a neighbor's house and the neighbor's pet mutt attacked the lad and bit him in the face. The dog then ran away, and along its way it bit a cow and 25 other dogs before it was caught up with and destroyed.

Holden volunteered to take Oscar to a Mad Stone, and after collecting a few dollars in donations from neighbors, he and the child set out for Columbia.

Once in Columbia with Oscar, Holden located a Dr. W. M, Biddle. Dr. Biddle possessed a Mad Stone owned by a man from Georgia. Biddle didn't think the Mad Stone would help the boy, but Holden was persistent, and Biddle reluctantly agreed to apply it. As it turned out, Holden didn't need the money he had raised. Dr. Biddle refused any payment for his services.

Biddle's Mad Stone, according to Holden, was about one and one-half inches long, and five-eighths of an inch wide. Biddle first placed the Mad Stone into warm water, and when it was cleansed, the doctor applied to little Oscar's wound. The Mad Stone gripped the wound with such strength that it drew blood.

The Mad Stone clung to the wound for 90 minutes before it released itself. Biddle soaked the Mad Stone in milk to remove the poison, and then he reapplied it. The process of application followed by the cleansing was repeated several times over a 12-hour period before the treatment was finally concluded.

After the treatment, Holden returned little Oscar to his home, and he told Oscar's parents that the boy was cured.

[Indiana] March 24, 1889. The Terre Haute Mad Stone was applied to the 11-year-old daughter of John Kirk, a Rush County, Indiana farmer. She was bitten on March 10, by a puppy which died after it displayed all the signs of hydrophobia.

The puppy also bit two of the girl's sisters, and it was thought to have scratched her four-year-old brother. The teeth marks on the girls weren't deep, but the skin was broken, and their wounds did bleed.

The stone adhered to the 11-year-old's wound for nearly 12 hours. The Mad Stone was "thoroughly saturated" and the cloth covering it was "soaked" with "poisonous looking matter." It was unusual for the Terra Haute Mad Stone to adhere to a wound for so long. The record was 14 hours, but that had happened many years before.

As soon as the Mad Stone dropped off, it was cleaned and applied to the boy's wounds but it didn't stick. This confirmed the supposition that his wound was a mere scratch.

On March 25, the Mad Stone was applied to the second girl, a five-year-old. It adhered to her wound for eight hours.

The Terre Haute Mad Stone was said to have "an authentic record" of more than 80 years, and it was purported to have worked in every instance. The owner stated he would keep some of the poison absorbed by the Mad Stone and submit it for scientific analysis.

[Indiana] March 25, 1889. The Terre Haute Mad Stone was popular. That evening, while the second Kirk girl was still in in treatment, two men from Warren County, Indiana came to have the Mad Stone applied to them.

The men were worried that they may have absorbed the rabies virus from getting a hog's saliva under their fingernails. The hog, and several others in the same pen had been bitten by a stray dog, and three of them had already died.

The mad dog was still running wild in Warren County.

[Georgia] April 3, 1889. The Lookout Valley area of northern Georgia, according to reports, was "overrun with mad dogs. The daughter of T. S. Miller, a farmer living near Gerber, Georgia was bitten. Two Mad Stones were applied to her wounds; one stuck, and one didn't.

Several other people had been bitten, and a "general slaughter" of dogs was underway.

[Georgia] April 10, 1889. Mr. M. Hair of Buena Vista, Marion County, Georgia had an unusually large "genuine madstone." He said his father had given it to him many years earlier. Hair said his father brought the Mad Stone from North Carolina in 1834.

Hair's Mad Stone was three-quarters of an inch thick, one and three-quarters inches wide, and two and one-quarter inches long. The Mad Stone was "slightly" oval shaped, was light gray, and was about as heavy as a normal stone.

Oddly, Hair had only recently realized that it was a Mad Stone. He became convinced after reading descriptions of other Mad Stones. Hair's father had used the Mad Stone to remove warts, but never to absorb rabies virus.

[Tennessee] April 17, 1889. Despite the medical profession's condemnation of Mad Stones, many people maintained an unshakeable faith in them. In fact, the use of Mad Stones appeared to be on the rise.

Mad Stone believers held to the proposition that scientists tended to discount or ignore those things they couldn't account for or didn't understand.

The scientists were certain that they did understand Mad Stones and that they could account for how Mad Stones worked. The consensus was that Mad Stones were worthless as a treatment for anything. The scientists doubted that Mad Stones would actually adhere to bite wounds, much less absorb the virus that caused rabies.

The medical community hypothesized that when Mad Stones seemed to work it was due to the placebo effect. In other words, believers wanted Mad Stones to work, therefore, they rationalized that they did work.

When patients died after Mad Stone treatments, those that believed in them attributed the failure to factors unrelated to the magical stone. Excuses included the contention that bite victims waited too long before getting treatment; the Mad Stone was applied incorrectly; or the practitioner wasn't using a "real" Mad

Stone. The list of failures was long, however, usually, the fact that a patient had died was never circulated widely.

There was also a group of people between the believers and the non-believers. These people conjectured that use of Mad Stones should continue even if they didn't work in every instance. These people contended that Mad Stones had the virtue of giving people with no chance of survival a modicum of hope, comfort, and peace of mind, even if only briefly.

[Tennessee] May 2, 1889. As related earlier in this volume, Mad Stones were occasionally used for snake bites. Here is one example:

Lafayette Cheatam lived near Adams in McNairy County. On May 2, a snake bit Cheatam's little son. The determination was made that the snake was a "water moccasin" (cottonmouth), and that medical treatment was necessary.

Instead of consulting a physician, Cheatham carried the child to Mad Stone practitioner. The practitioner applied a Mad Stone "with good effect." Cheatham said that after receiving the Mad Stone treatment, the boy "suffered but little."

[Kentucky] May 5, 1889. Bert Curtis, an 18-year-old farm boy from Mt. Sterling, Kentucky, died from hydrophobia. The details of what happened were unusual. Sometime before, Curtis and a cousin were engaging in horseplay when the farm's watchdog charged at them, and bit them both. The dog was determined to be rabid.

The cousins had their wounds cauterized and then they had Mad Stones applied. The Mad Stone adhered to Curtis, but not to his cousin. The Mad Stone drew "considerable greenish fluid" from the young farmer's wound.

Despite his medical treatment and the application of the Mad Stone, Curtis became ill on April 28, and he was in great agony for the next week before he finally expired.

[Tennessee] June 13, 1889. There were those determined to convince doubters that Mad Stones were real, whether they worked or not. A man living in Georgia named William Vanvalkenburg was in Nashville visiting his brother, G. S. Vanvalkenburg. While in the city, William went to the offices of the *Daily American* and left his Mad Stone with the newspaper's editor. He said he would allow the editor to examine the Mad Stone for a few days, then he would retrieve it before he returned to Georgia.

Vanvalkenburg said he had kept the stone as a curiosity for almost three decades. He said the Mad Stone was "taken from a large antlered buck killed in Irwin County, Georgia in the summer of 1860. The Mad Stone was found "encysted or enclosed by a grisly substance, which was attached inside the pouch, close to the entrance of the esophagus or gullet" of the deer.

According to Vanvalkenburg, the man who killed the deer was old, and he had been taught to extract Mad Stones by Native Americans. The old man said he never killed a deer without searching for the "Benzel," which is what he called Mad Stones. The old man had related that he only found one Mad Stone for about every 200 deer he killed.

The old man was not alone. For many years deer hunters took the time to search for a Mad Stone in the internal tracts and bladders of each magnificent animal they felled. Mad Stones taken from white deer were considered of superior quality, but the carcasses of other deer were searched as well.

Vanvalkenburg's Mad Stone was oval shaped, was one and one-half inches long, one inch wide, and five-eighths of an inch thick. Unlike most Mad Stones, this one was of a "yellowish gray color" and it wasn't layered like a slate rock.

Vanvalkenburg stated that he had no opinion as to whether Mad Stones worked or not. However, Vanvalkenburg spoke of "authenticated accounts" of Mad Stones being successfully used in Virginia and Georgia.

[Missouri] June 18, 1889. Dr. Ed Small, Chief Surgeon of the Missouri, Kansas & Texas Railroad, had a problem with the Mad Stone myth. He issued a challenge to R. A. Blair and Dr. T. E. White. Blair and White of Sedalia, Missouri had Mad Stones they claimed were "sure antidotes for mad dog bites."

Small stated his view that Mad Stones possessed "no virtues whatsoever," and he was willing to wager $500 to prove it. Small offered that amount to anyone willing to submit to being bitten by a mad dog, followed by a Mad Stone application. If the Mad Stone worked, the subject would be healthy and $500 richer. If it didn't the subject, the $500 could pay for his funeral.

[Kentucky] August 1, 1889. Joseph McMillian, a farmer from Webster County, Kentucky killed a mad dog that had bitten him. McMillian was in so much pain that he went to Henderson, Kentucky to be treated with a Mad Stone.

The Mad Stone stuck to McMillian's wound, and eventually it had to be pulled off. It was reapplied several times until it was thought to have removed all the poison.

[Illinois] August 14, 1889. T. M. Orton, a wealthy farmer from Denver, Hancock County, Illinois owned a Mad Stone. He related that he believed it "instrumental" in saving many lives.

The Orton Mad Stone was bigger than most. It was four inches long, three and one-half inches wide, and it weighed close to a pound. The Mad Stone looked like a "petrified honeycomb," but it was more like a piece of coral. The curious stone was porous, and when it was placed in water or milk, the fluid bubbled through it furiously. Yet, the Mad Stone never softened.

Orton was a native of Madison County, Kentucky, and it was there that he acquired the Mad Stone.

According to Orton, about 1829, a wealthy old man named Hoagland moved to Madison County, and he brought the Mad Stone with him. Hoagland told his new neighbors that he believed the Mad Stone came from some "remote part of the South."

Hoagland continued that a slave woman in Louisiana told him many "wonderful stories of miracles that had been performed with the Mad Stone."

The Mad Stone, so said Hoagland, had cured many people bitten by mad dogs, poisonous snakes, and other reptiles. But more that, it had also been put to clever use in driving away witches. But Hoagland himself never applied the Mad Stone in Madison County.

Hoagland didn't place much value, at least not momentarily, on the Mad Stone. He gave it to his school aged son who was a classmate of Orton's. Orton became fascinated by the Mad Stone and he traded his prized jackknife for it.

Rabies had never been a major problem in Madison County, but one day a mad dog bit an African American girl. Orton was determined to save the girl's life and he applied the Mad Stone in Madison County for the first time.

When Orton placed the Mad Stone on the girl's wound, she mentioned a "severe drawing sensation" which increased and decreased from time to time as if it were pulsating. The girl recovered completely and never developed any symptoms of hydrophobia.

Orton applied the Mad Stone in Kentucky several other times, and the results were always positive.

Orton moved his family to Hancock County, Illinois in 1856. Over the next three decades and change, he had, according to his statements, applied the Mad Stone 25 to 30 times to those bitten by venomous snakes or mad dogs. He claimed that in every case, his "patients" had recovered.

He said he didn't keep a record of his Mad Stone applications, but Orton could recount his most memorable cases:

Orton related the story of a young man who came from Kansas in 1887 to get treatment. The man had been bitten badly through the wrist by a rabid canine. The dog had also bitten some cattle, and they had died from hydrophobia. Orton applied the Mad Stone to the Jayhawker and it adhered immediately. A few minutes later, a stream of blood, water, and "putrid matter" ran through the Mad Stone and shot out shot onto the floor.

Then he related the story of a patient whose enormous swelling in his arm from a dog bite was reduced in a matter of minutes.

Orton was a busy Mad Stone applicator. So far in the summer of 1889, he had treated six people:

Charles Huey, a boy from St. Mary's Township who had been bitten by a mad dog.

William Parker, an old man from Kellerville, Illinois. He suffered from a mad dog bite.

Ira Punty, a boy from Carthage, Illinois, who had been bitten by a rabid dog.

Clara Rice, a little girl from Piper City, Illinois who had been bitten by a rabid cat.

Charles T. Floyd, a little boy from Meredosia, Illinois, who was bitten by a mad dog.

G. W. E. Cook, ex-Mayor of Lacon, Illinois, who suffered from a mad dog bite. The Cook case became well-known.

Cook owned two valuable dogs, a St. Bernard, and an English pug. He was supervising some work being done on his property, and he had his two dogs with him.

Suddenly, a stray dog appeared in the road running toward Cook and his dogs. The dog was drooling profusely and snapping at everything in its path. Cook protected his dogs by sending them into the house, but he couldn't avoid the rabid dog. The vicious canine bit him on the hand in two places.

The former mayor went to Orton and Orton applied his Mad Stone. The Mad Stone adhered tightly.

The feeling Orton's Mad Stone produced surprised Cook. He said, "It acts as if it were alive." Then within minutes, the former mayor turned extremely pale and murmured softly, "The drawing sensation makes me sick."

Orton explained it was normal for patients to experience "excessive nausea."

Cook left after the session believing he was cured.

Orton's procedure for treating his patients never varied:

1. A doctor usually attended the session and "scarified" the wound before Orton applied the Mad Stone.
2. The Mad Stone was cleansed thoroughly by boiling it in water and milk before Orton applied it.
3. The concave side of the Mad Stone was then placed on the wound.
4. As long as the patient felt the drawing sensation, the Mad Stone was left attached.
5. After being removed, the Mad Stone was cleansed again, and it was ready for a reuse.

Orton said that when the Mad Stone was first removed, it displayed "no indication of having absorbed any poisonous matter." However, when the Mad Stone was boiled in water and milk after the treatment, a "green scum" rose to the service. The green slime was believed to contain the rabies virus, and Orton was extremely cautious about handling the vessel holding it. In fact, he used a special pot for boiling the Mad Stone.

Despite his stories about the Mad Stone's power to cure his patients, Orton's opinion of it was strange. He said, "I confess I have been skeptical as to its virtues. I don't know why it should heal these wounds, yet it has done so in every instance. There must be something in it, but I cannot explain it to you.

Dr. J. J. Reaburn also lived in Denver, Illinois. Even though he was a medical professional, he didn't dismiss Orton's Mad Stone as mere superstition. The doctor said, "I have not studied the question thoroughly. I would like to have the opinion of some eminent geologist on the subject. It may be that there are great virtues in the stone. I have watched it operate. It may be a coral. It may possibly belong to the Silurian Age. There can be no doubt that it has saved the lives of many persons bitten by rabid animals."

[Tennessee] November 23, 1889. Two little girls from Dayton, Floria Morrison and Ida Spence, were playing with a pet cat. Suddenly, the cat "flew" at Floria and bit her on the shoulder. Then the feline turned its attention to Ida and bit her in the face. The cat was killed immediately after attacking the girls.

Ida was suffering from intense pain and a messenger was sent to Chattanooga to retrieve a Mad Stone.

[Tennessee] December 10, 1889. About 10 a.m. on an early December morning in Hampshire, Maury County, Mrs. David Patterson was stooping over a washtub when a mad dog came up behind her. As she turned, the dog lunged at her, and it clinched her left arm between its teeth. The dog bit Patterson twice and it took all the power she could muster to break away from the vicious brute.

T. W. Patton and James Nowles transported Patterson to Columbia where they stopped at the home of F. A. Watson. Watson sent for Dr. W. M. Biddle who arrived shortly thereafter with his Mad Stone.

Biddle remained skeptical of the Mad Stone's value as a treatment, and he doubted that the dog was rabid. Yet, he took his Mad Stone, which was about the size of a "chew of plug tobacco," and applied it to Patterson's wounds. The Mad Stone adhered to the worst of Patterson's wounds and remained affixed for about 10 minutes. However, it didn't stick to the other wounds at all.

Uncertain that Biddle's Mad Stone had cured her, Patterson remained overnight in Columbia and then began to look elsewhere for a better Mad Stone practitioner. Eventually, Patterson and her entourage traveled to Nashville's Edgefield district and located the renowned Alexander Joseph and his Mad Stone.

According to her companions, by the time Patterson arrived at the Joseph home, her arm was swollen to double its normal size, and her "eyes were almost bursting from their sockets. Her entire system was terribly deranged, and her nervous system was almost entirely undermined."

Virginia Joseph, who was originally from North Carolina, treated as many patients as her husband did. At about 9 a.m. on December 13, Virginia began treating Patterson. By 1:30 p.m., Patterson's swelling had virtually vanished, and her eyes had returned to normal.

Saying she felt like a new woman, Patterson returned home. She was certain that she was cured.

Virginia Joseph was proud of her work. She beamed when she spoke of her two most celebrated cases:

In the first case, an African American man had been bitten by a "venomous reptile." The man's face had enlarged, and his eyes were enflamed and almost swollen shut. Virginia applied the Mad Stone to the man's wounds, and it cured him immediately.

In the other case, two boys were bitten by a rabid dog and were on the "verge of spasms from hydrophobia." The boys were in intense pain, but as soon as the Mad Stone was applied, they were "quieted and reduced to a normal condition."

The latest story concerning the origins of the Joseph Mad Stone was that it was 120 years old. It was found by the "seashore" of an unidentified state (probably North Carolina), by an ancestor of a Colonel Peters. Then, years after Peters came in possession of it, a "scientist" told him of the Mad Stone's value in treating mad dog bites. Since then, the Mad Stone had "effective a number of marvelous cures."

The Joseph's Mad Stone was characterized as being of a "distinctly" oval shape. It was "exceedingly porous and finely grained." It was about one and one-half inches wide, one-half inch thick, two inches long, and very heavy for its size. The Mad Stone was black on its ends, allegedly from being in contact with wounds.

Virginia Joseph said that "several eminent scientists had examined it," but that they couldn't determine the Mad Stone's composition.

The Joseph method of Mad Stone treatment followed a formalized regimen:
1. Bathe the wound.
2. Bandage the Mad Stone to the wound.
3. Allow the Mad Stone to draw the poison from the wound.
4. After the Mad Stone has ceased to absorb poison, remove it from the wound.
5. Place the Mad Stone in warm water (or warm milk). The Mad Stone will sizzle as if it was hot and the liquid was ice cold.
6. When the poison has exited the Mad Stone, it is ready for reuse.

Observers stated that when the Mad Stone was submerged in milk after being removed from a wound, it would discharge the rabies virus which would rise to the top. The virus could be identified easily from its "sickly green" color.

1890

[Tennessee] January 26, 1890. Monroe Driver, who lived in Cumberland County about eight miles southwest of Crossville, possessed a Mad Stone. He said he took it from the stomach of a deer he killed about 1878. He continued that in about 1880, a rabid dog bit his young daughter. Driver pulled out his Mad Stone and applied it to his little daughter's wound, and it adhered to the teeth marks.

The incident proved in Driver's mind that his Mad Stone could not fail. His indisputable evidence was that his daughter never developed symptoms of hydrophobia.

Driver wanted to benefit others. He said he would treat anyone who needed his help.

[Tennessee] January 27, 1890. James Baugh Dinwiddie of Henry County reminded the public that he had a Mad Stone. Dinwiddie said the marvelous rabies preventative had been in family for 75 years, and that it had been applied successfully hundreds of times. Moreover, Dinwiddie stated that his Mad Stone had "never been known to fail."

[Tennessee] April 3, 1890. Dr. Levin Dickson Wright was a dentist living in Dickson, Tennessee. However, Wright wasn't known for yanking teeth as much as he was for his Mad Stone. He said his Mad Stone had "stood many tests and has never failed to effect a cure."

Wright described his Mad Stone as "small, of a peculiar color, and very porous."

The story went that the Mad Stone was purchased in the West Indies by Reverend W. H. Adcock sometime before 1840. After keeping the Mad Stone for 20 or more years, Adcock gave it to Dr. Wright.

Wright had applied his Mad Stone to patients from Dickson, Humphries, Cheatham, Montgomery, and Davidson counties. One of his most memorial treatments was in the case of Tom Simpkins' child. The Simpkins family lived on Whites Creek in Davidson County. The child was "terribly lacerated by a rabid dog." However, Wright applied his Mad Stone and it extracted the virus "from the wounds after several applications."

[Tennessee] April 3, 1890. Dr. Levin Dickson Wright was tasked to use his Mad Stone again.

D. E. Spenser who lived 10 miles south of Dickson at Spencer's Mill was walking down the public road near his home. Suddenly, a mad dog appeared and attacked him. The animal tore at Spenser, biting him five times (thrice on one the arm, and twice on one leg).

The dog then staggered down the road to the farm owned by Spencer's brother. There, it became aggressive again. It bit two dogs and several geese before Spencer's brother shot and killed it.

No one could identify the dog or say where it came from. This led to the presumption that it had rabies.

Fearing that he had to act before he suffered sure death from hydrophobia, Spencer went immediately to Dr. Wright's residence. Wright applied his Mad Stone to each of Spencer's wounds, one after another, several times until his miracle stone no longer adhered to any of them.

Still worried, on April 5, Spencer returned for another round of treatment. This time, the Mad Stone would only stick to one wound, and then, only for a minute or so.

Spenser left the dentist's home satisfied that "the little West Indian Stone had saved him from a horrible death of hydrophobia."

[Tennessee] April 5, 1890. A Mrs. Smiley of Ridgetop, in Robertson County, was bitten by a dog suspected of having rabies. She went to Edgefield and Alexander Joseph's Mad Stone was applied to her wound.

[Kentucky] April 20, 1890. W. J. Isbell was dying from what his doctor, J. J. Jepson, said was "genuine rabies." Isbell was suffering from constant convulsions, and he was expected to be dead in a few days.

Isbell was a wealthy farmer living in Warren County, Kentucky about 10 miles from Bowling Green. He had been feeding his livestock in early March when one of his dogs attacked one of his hogs. Isbell attempted to stop the attack, but the dog turned on him and bit him through the thumb.

About 10 days after the incident, the wounded hog went into convulsions and died. The hog's death alarmed Isbell and he had a Mad Stone applied to his wound. He was comforted by the fact that he appeared to be free of rabies. Then about April 13, Isbell's hand and arm began to swell, and he experienced great pain.

He waited until the morning of April 18, and then he had another Mad Stone application. Later that evening, he began to have trouble swallowing. The next day, he attempted to drink water, but he went into a spasm. Isbell was extremely thirsty, but he was unable to drink water, or anything else.

Dr. Jepson ran a rubber tube into Isbell's mouth and forced a few drops of water down the tormented man's throat, but it only caused Isbell to have another convulsion. By April 20, Isbell couldn't even swallow his own saliva.

[Tennessee] December 25, 1890. Mattie Merritt was a single woman who lived with her widowed mother about three miles from the Franklin County town of Decherd. On Christmas Day, a "yellow cur" came into her house and it bit her through the hand.

She showed no signs of any problem from the bite until March 2, 1891, when the telltale signs of hydrophobia appeared in the form of convulsions.

Dr. King, and Dr. Cherry, both of Decherd, attempted to treat Merritt, but they couldn't help her. Then, in desperation, she received treatment with a Mad Stone. However, the Mad Stone provided her with no relief. On March 7, 1891, Merritt's agony ended when she died.

An older African American woman was bitten by the same dog that bit Merritt, but she was fortunate in that she never developed any symptoms of rabies.

Chapter Sources:

"A Genuine Madstone." *The Daily American*, August 14, 1889.

"A Georgia Mad Stone." *The Daily American*, April 10, 1889.

"Applying the Madstone." *The Daily American*, March 27, 1889.

"A Real, Genuine Madstone." *The Daily American*, June 14, 1889.

"A Wonderful Madstone." *The Daily American*, January 26, 1890.

"Bitten by a Mad Dog." *The Daily American*, December 12, 1889.

"Bolivar." *The Daily American*, June 17, 1886.

"Brief Telegrams." *The Daily American*, January 3, 1886.

"Cured by a Madstone." *The Daily American*, February 16, 1889.

"Cured by a Madstone." *The Daily American*, February 26, 1888.

"Cured the Rabies." *The Daily American*, December 13, 1889.

"Death from Hydrophobia." *The Daily American*, February 22, 1887.

"Died of Hydrophobia." *The Daily American*, August 27, 1886.

"Died of Hydrophobia." *The Daily American*, May 7, 1889.

"Died of Hydrophobia." *The Daily American*, July 14, 1888.

"Dog Days are Here." *The Daily American*, July 25, 1888.

"Franklin, Ky." *The Daily American*, March 13, 1886.

"Gleanings from the State Press." *The Daily American*, November 23, 1888.

"He Has a Madstone." *The Daily American*, January 27, 1890.

"History of a Madstone." *The Daily American*, March 25, 1889.

"In Tennessee Towns." *The Daily American*, May 6, 1889.

"Lynchburg." *The Daily American*, January 26, 1886.

"Madstone's Efficacy." *The Daily American*, April 6, 1890.

"Many Mad Dogs." *The Daily American*, April 4, 1889.

"Men Who Have Faith in Mad Stones Given a Chance." *The Daily American*, June 19, 1889.

"Minor Local Mention." *The Daily American*, April 12, 1890.

"Over the State." *The Daily American*, April 17, 1887.

"Rabies and the Madstone." *The Daily American*, April 17, 1889.

"Rather Queer Proposition." *The Daily American*, June 19, 1889.

"Ravages of a Mad Dog." *The Daily American*, March 20, 1888.

"Real Madstone." *The Daily American*, September 24, 1886.

"Testing Its Virtues." *The Daily American*, August 2, 1889.

"The Deadly Mad Dog." *The Daily American*, July 24, 1888.

"The Madstone of No Avail." *The Daily American*, March 11, 1891.

"Victim of Rabies." *The Daily American*, April 21, 1890.

"Widespread Alarm." *The Daily American*, March 16, 1887.

5. 1891-1895

1891

[Tennessee] April 27, 1891. A two-year-old boy died from the effects of hydrophobia. The toddler was the son of Frank M. Trenary. of Lischey Avenue near the Nashville city limits.

Around the beginning of April, the boy was playing near his home when a large shepherd dog attacked him. The dog, which belonged to a neighbor referred to Mrs. Cleveland, ripped at the boy's throat, and left severe wounds on his neck.

The attack happened at about 11 a.m., and at about 2 p.m., Trenary took the boy to Alexander Joseph for a Mad Stone treatment. The treatment was merely precautionary, as the dog had shown no previous signs of rabies.

Joseph applied the Mad Stone to the boy's neck, and it held on for two hours. When the Mad Stone fell away, it left "an angry red place" as if "blood had been drawn" away from the wound "by force."

Those who claimed to understand the workings of the mythical Mad Stone pronounced themselves "perfectly satisfied" that Joseph's Mad Stone had accomplished its purpose. They were confident that the boy was cured.

Not wishing to take any chances, Trenary carried the boy to the family physician. Dr. D. L. Arrington. Arrington followed the routine procedure in possible hydrophobia cases and cauterized the wound.

Despite the boy's constant "picking" at it, the wound healed quickly, and his parents felt that the danger had been avoided. However, his doctor knew better.

Throughout the week after the attack, Dr. Arrington saw the boy several times, and he suspected that the child "was not right." However, Arrington didn't reveal his suspicions to the boy's parents. He felt that doing so "could do no good, and that it might cause harm by unnecessarily alarming the parents."

By April 24, the boy's wounds had healed completely, However, on that very day, he became "very nervous." His parents, not considering that the dog bite might have something to do with the boy's behavior, did not send for Dr. Arrington. The boy didn't sleep that night, and the next morning he began spitting up a pink substance.

Dr. Arrington came to the Trenary home on the morning of April 26. He found the boy "running around the room like a caged tiger." The boy's eyes were glazed, and although he seemed to recognize those around him, he was afraid of being approached.

Arrington noticed that the child displayed other symptoms of rabies as well. A light red foam dripped from the boy's mouth, and he suffered from sporadic convulsions. At Frank Trenary's suggestion, the doctor inspected the child's tongue and it appeared to be normal.

With Arrington expressing doubts about curing the boy, Frank Trenary decided to have the Mad Stone applied again. He set the date of the application for April 28. The second Mad Stone treatment never occurred, however.

On April 27, doctors Arrington and W. G. Ewing came to the Trenary home and they observed the child running around the room just as he had been doing on the previous day. The boy was even more nervous and his foaming at the mouth had increased.

The tortured toddler had coughing fits every few minutes. The sounds he made during the fits were like nothing the doctors had ever heard before. The coughing began "with a harsh hack" and ended "with the sound of a thick fluid."

The youngster would grab bread, crackers, and other food, and eat it "ravenously" only "to throw it up again immediately."

The doctors did all they could do, which wasn't much. They departed the house knowing the situation was hopeless.

In his last hours, the child would run around the room, then he'd fall down glaring at his helpless parents through glazed eyes. Between 10 and 11 a.m. on April 27, the boy had one last spasm and then he died.

[Tennessee] May 26, 1891. Allen Gunn of Tullahoma had a five-month-old bird dog which bit several people. Those bitten by the dog included Gunn, two of his children, two of James Anderson's children, and one of Tom Mangrom's children.

Allen tied up the puppy and it was soon observed it having fits. Locals knowledgeable of rabies declared the puppy was suffering from hydrophobia, prompting Allen to kill it.

The parents of those bitten had delayed in getting treatment for their children until they were certain that the dog was rabid. When they became certain, the fear among them grew that they had waited too long.

A frantic search ended when a Mad Stone practitioner was near Manchester. He applied his Mad Stone to each of the children, and it adhered to each of them for a duration of four and one-half to ten hours.

[Alabama] June 24, 1891. Word from Eufaula, Barbour County, Alabama was that a mad dog was roaming around there. It had bitten its owner, B. P. Mckennzie, and McKennzie had taken a Mad Stone treatment.

The story went that "Eufaula is in great glee. Not every community can own a Mad Stone."

[Tennessee] July 28, 1891. A Mrs. Sherrill of Shelbyville, and her daughter were both bitten by a dog suspected of being rabid. They came to Davidson County and paid a visit to the locally famous Mad Stone practitioner, Alexander Joseph.

Joseph applied the Mad Stone to their wounds until it ceased to adhere. After the treatment, they returned to Shelbyville satisfied that they were no longer in danger.

[Tennessee] August 7, 1891. Nashville's "canine nuisance" was growing. After dark, dogs owned alleyways, side streets, and even some major thoroughfares. During the evening of August 7, 11 dogs engaged in a major fight on Cherry Street that stretched from Union to Church streets.

The situation was so serious that people on foot more often than not abandoned the sidewalks to aggressive dogs and walked in the muddy streets.

With the likelihood of a major outbreak of hydrophobia on the horizon, a number of citizens were taking the preemptively seeking out Mad Stones, just in the case that they needed one later.

1892

[Kentucky and Tennessee] April 6, 1892. Wash Rose of near Pembroke, Christian County, Kentucky, took his 7-year-old son to Nashville for a Mad Stone application. A family pet bit the boy. After attacking the child, the dog bit cows, horses, and hogs before it was "run down and killed." Despite its rampage, it wasn't determined that the dog suffered from hydrophobia until long after it bit the Rose child.

There was great concern in the community that the dog had bitten other people before being shot.

1893

[Tennessee] January 13, 1893. There was great "excitement" in the Smith County community of Riddleton. The belief was that hydrophobia was blazing through the area.

On January 12, a mad dog was killed in the area. Then, on the next day, a dog belonging to Dr. W. H. Jolly attacked Eugene Kindred. While battling with the dog, Kindred fell over a stone fence. Kindred suffered an injured hand, but he wasn't certain if it was hurt in his fall, or if the dog bit him. Kindred had a Mad Stone applied to his wound for safety's sake.

The marauding dog, and four others that it bit were destroyed. Beyond that, several other dogs were confined, to be killed if they developed hydrophobia.

The good folk of Riddleton expressed the belief that they wanted and needed "fewer dogs and more sheep." They asked the legislature to enact a law "by which children and sheep can be protected from the ravages of canines."

[Tennessee] April 22, 1893. Daisy Dobbins received a bad bite on her right arm by a rabid dog. Daisy was the 10-year-old daughter of Tom M. Dobbins who lived on Dobbins Pike about three miles northwest of Gallatin in Sumner County.

Daisy remained in intense pain from the bite, and a few days later, Dobbins called in Dr. Bush. Bush dressed the wound, but he thought a Mad Stone application might also help her. He suggested that Dobbins immediately take Daisy to Peter Henley at Shackle Island who had a Mad Stone. Henley applied the Mad Stone to Daisey's arm on April 24.

As for the dog that bit Daisey, it roamed to the Shiloh area, and bit livestock along his way until it was finally located and killed near Rogana.

[Tennessee and Mississippi] May 9, 1893. During the afternoon, two little daughters of Mrs. R. A. Johnsey of Jackson, Tennessee, were bitten by a dog suspected of being rabid. The girls were Elsie, age 4, and Alice, age 12.

The children were crossing the street from the corner grocery, Kunz's Store, intending to return to their home at 190 Highland Avenue. The girls were about in the middle of the street when a big, black hound dog pounced on upon Elise and her face was "horribly lacerated" by the fangs of the infuriated beast, and she was "dangerously injured." Elsie suffered two ugly gashes on her cheek, across her nose, and in the corner of one eye.

Alice Johnsey rescued her sister, but she was bitten through the lower lip in the process.

The two children were taken home where doctors McCoy and Booth dressed their wounds. By May 11, Elise could sit up in bed, but her wounds were bleeding through her bandages.

The mother of the girls, "frantic with grief and fright," wanted her daughters treated with a Mad Stone. P. F. Wilkerson, who lived fewer than 30 miles away in Bolivar, happened to be in Jackson. He said that when he went home, he would get the Mad Stone belonging to Miss Carraway and bring it back to Jackson, where he'd apply it to the children.

Mrs. Johnsey didn't want to wait for Wilkerson. She packed up the girls, and on the afternoon of May 13, she started off with them on a trip of about 100 miles to Blue Springs, Mississippi. There was a "famous" Mad Stone at Blue Springs, and Mrs. Johnsey hoped it would save her precious little girls.

1894

[Alabama and Tennessee] February 20, 1894. A dog suspected of being rabid bit Jane Miller who lived in Kendall, Lauderdale County, Alabama. A few days later she was transported to Tennessee to have a Mad Stone applied to her wound.

[Tennessee] July 20, 1894. Samuel N. Wantland of Carter's Creek, Maury County, came to Nashville to have a Mad Stone applied to his sons, William, age 3, and Henry, age 9. A mad dog had bitten the boys at their home on July 16. Their wounds were on their heads and faces.

The Wantland family spent the day at the home of Alexander Joseph, and the Mad Stone was applied with "most satisfactory results."

The boys were said to have been "much benefitted by the treatment." They returned home after being declared cured.

1895

[Tennessee] May 9, 1895. Hydrophobia was raging in Cheatham County. In the past two days, three mad dogs had been killed at Kingston Springs. Town residents were "constantly on the lookout for these terrible enemies of man and beast."

A few weeks earlier, a man named William Lampley living west of Kingston Springs was bitten by a dog thought to be rabid. Lampley died just days after "displaying undoubted symptoms of hydrophobia."

A neighbor of Lampley's named Fred Palmore had a son bitten by a stray dog. Not wanting his son to suffer the same fate as Lampley, Palmore took the boy to Dickson and had a Mad Stone applied to the youngster's wounds. The Mad Stone stuck to the bitten area several times.

A few miles north of Kingston Sprigs at Dock Creek, farmers had killed a number of suspected rabid dogs that had attacked livestock.

On May 9, Jesse Ham and Sam Brown shot gunned a pack of mad dogs led by a "very large" and "very ferocious" animal. The dogs were rushing toward a group of unarmed plowmen, and the belief was that if Ham and Brown had not been present, the attacking dogs would have injured one or more of the farm hands.

The truth is that rabid animals do not run in packs, therefore, the pack of animals threatening the plowmen were not rabid. Naturally, they may have been infected, but there was no way of knowing that.

Chapter Sources:

"Bitten by a Mad Dog." *The Daily American*, April 8, 1892.

"Bitten by a Mad Dog." *The Daily American*, April 25, 1893.

"Bitten by a Mad Dog." *The Daily American*, May 10, 1893.

"In Alabama." *The Daily American*, June 24, 1891.

"Mad Stone Applied." *The Daily American*, August 3, 1891.

"Over the State." *The Daily American*, May 12, 1893.

"Rabid Dogs." *The Daily American*, January 16, 1893.

"Supposed to be a Mad Dog." *The Daily American*, February 27, 1894.

"Tennessee in Type." *The Daily American*, June 1, 1891.

"The Dog Nuisance." *The Daily American*, August 8, 1891.

"The Madstone Failed." *The Daily American*, April 28, 1891.

"To Try Mad Stone." *The Daily American*, May 14, 1893.

"Tried the Madstone." *The Daily American*, July 20, 1894.

"Work of Mad Dogs." *The Nashville American*, May 10, 1895.

6. 1896-1900

1896

[Tennessee] April 17, 1896. A suspected mad dog bit Willie Shofner, the son of prominent Wartrace miller, T. A. Shofner. Since the dog was at large, it was impossible to know if it was rabid.

Shofner wanted to take no chances. He carried his son to Fairfield immediately and had Watt Clark apply his Mad Stone. The Mad Stone adhered to Willie's wound for several hours.

[Tennessee] June 2, 1896. Two small children belonging to F. P. Randolph of Montgomery County, were bitten by a bird dog. It was thought to be rabid. The offending pooch had been bitten about two weeks before by a mad dog that also attacked several cattle and other farm animals.

Randolph was in Clarksville on June 3, searching for someone with a Mad Stone.

[Tennessee] June 15, 1896. John Smith lived on Shipman's Creek in Bedford County, four miles from Normandy. His four-year-old son, Floy, was bitten by a feist dog. The dog began to have "mad fits" and it was killed. The boy's wound healed quickly, and the dog bite was forgotten almost as quickly.

Then, on about July 6, spasms suddenly seized the child. Smith called in a physician who took no time in diagnosing the child as suffering from hydrophobia. The doctor cautioned the boy's family members not to allow the child to bite or scratch any of them. But somehow, Floy bit his mother and his aunt, Mrs. Matt Smith.

The child bit his mother several times on the breast and arm. The bites were so severe that the doctor felt it was certain that the rabies virus entered her body. Smith's wound wasn't as serious, and it was thought unlikely that she was in any danger of contracting hydrophobia.

The child died on July 12, and his mother was so filled with "grief over the death of her only child" that she longed for death herself. However, her husband forced her to allow a Mad Stone to be applied to her wounds. Despite the Mad Stone treatment, the distraught was expected to die.

[Tennessee] August 4, 1896. A Mr. Berry of Dowelltown, and Robert Roper of Alexandria were bitten by a mad dog at Brush Creek. It wasn't certain that the dog was rabid, but the assumption was that it was. This was because that a number of the dogs and hogs in the area had died from the "dreaded disease" in the weeks before the men were bitten.

Berry traveled to Woodbury and received the Mad Stone treatment. The Mad Stone adhered to his wound for a full eight hours.

Roper went to Grant, in Smith County and received a Mad Stone application there. The Mad Stone stuck to his wound for four hours.

As of August 11, both men were reportedly doing well.

[Kentucky] November 27, 1896. A mad dog bit John Adams of Somerset, Pulaski County, Kentucky on the hand. Shortly after being bitten, instead of seeking out medical assistance Adams tried to cauterize the wound himself. He used the end of a stick he had charred over an open flame. He burnt his hand badly making his wound worse.

After his failed attempt to treat himself, Adams was taken to Stanford, Lincoln County, Kentucky to receive the application of the "Dudderar Mad Stones." They were applied to the wound and they adhered.

The Dudderar Mad Stones had gained fame throughout Kentucky and Tennessee. The owner said they were brought from Missouri to Kentucky in 1842 by his father, Samuel Dudderar. Samuel Dudderar had contended that they came from the gullet of a Rocky Mountain goat. The story was that in the more than half of a century that the Dudderar family had possessed the Mad Stones, they had been applied in more than 1,000 dog bite cases, and they had succeeded in every case except one. In that case death occurred because, according to Dudderar, "the wound was neglected for 18 days after the biting."

1897

[Tennessee] May 4, 1897. The Upper Cumberland Medical Society met in convention at the resort town of Bloomington Springs in Putnam County. Several of the physicians presented demonstrations and papers on many current topics of medical interest.

The Mad Stone wasn't neglected at the conference. Dr. A. J. McClarney of Crossville presented a demonstration to his fellows called an "Exhibition of Mad Stone."

[Tennessee] June 17, 1897. A dog bit two visitors to Nashville on West End Avenue. The dog threatened to go on a rampage before a police officer named Cummings killed it. The dog, a Fox Terrier, was first sighted near the corner of West End Avenue and Belmont.

The two men weren't familiar with Nashville. One was an older gentleman. He was bitten several times on both legs.

The other man was somewhat younger than companion. He suffered a serious gash on one leg.

The men went to the Demoville & Company store on the corner of Church and Cherry Streets where they inquired about purchasing a Mad Stone. The store stocked many medicines and remedies, including the famous mineral water from Red Boiling Springs. However, it didn't carry Mad Stones.

The disappointed men departed the store, and the city, without giving anyone their names.

[Tennessee] November 16, 1897. The news was that a mad dog attack in Dickson resulted in the victim having a Mad Stone applied. There was no word as to the bitten person's name, or whether the Mad Stone adhered or not.

1898

[Alabama] January 4, 1898. Martin Webster, a boy of 15 who lived with his parents in West Huntsville, was bitten by a mad dog. Martin had found a stray and had brought it home to make it a pet. Martin and his mom were feeding the dog "when it was seized with a fit of rabies and attacked them." The woman avoided the dog's lunges, but the dog ripped open the teenager's arm.

Martin was carried into the Huntsville on January 5, and a Mad Stone was applied.

[Alabama] April 19, 1898. There was a mad dog scare in Athens, Alabama. That morning, a dog belonging to DeWitt Calvin went mad and bit a dog and a cow, then it bit Calvin's small son on the hand. The attack so frightened the boy that he ran away and hid. By that afternoon, his family still hadn't found him.

The dog was killed without it ever being determined whether it actually had rabies.

While the search for the child continued, Calvin sent an older son to procure a Mad Stone.

[Tennessee] July 5, 1898. Mad dogs were rampant in White County. Or at least, many residents there believed they were.

A merchant named Winstead who lived in the community of Walling was returning from hunting with his son and his dog. As he approached his home he came upon a mad dog that had already bitten some of his dogs and hogs.

Winstead's hunting dog and the mad dog began fighting, and Winstead open fire. After being bitten, Winstead's dog became confused and it turned and bit its master on the hand.

Although bitten by his own dog, Winstead kept after the mad dog. Finally, after knocking the vicious animal down several times and shooting it seven times, he killed the mad dog.

Winstead had a Mad Stone applied to his injury, and it adhered to his hand. However, he wasn't satisfied with the treatment he received, and he passed through McMinnville seeking another Mad Stone. He found one and the Mad Stone stuck to his mangled hand three times.

[Virginia] November 12, 1898. Mad Stones were valuable, so it should come as no surprise that there were lawsuits over their ownership from time to time. In Leesburg, Virginia there was a court battle over the state's most famous Mad Stone. This stone, according to the litigants, had been "heralded for more than a century."

The Leesburg Mad Stone was set to be sold in December after a lawsuit between three claimants to it was settled by a court decree. Until then it was being held at the Loudoun National Bank in Leesburg. Those with claims had been two nephews and a niece of the late Mrs. Fred. The litigants were nephews Mr. Seaton, and Mr. Triplet, and niece, Mrs. German. Several of the Old Dominion's best-known attorneys argued the case. One of them was Eppa Hunton Jr., the son of the former Confederate General and United States Senator, Eppa Hunton Sr. Mrs. German won the case.

The Leesburg Mad Stone, thought by some to be more precious than gold, wasn't very impressive looking. It was chocolate colored, two inches long, one inch wide, and one-half thick. It had a silver band holding it together because it had been broken several times.

The legend was that the Leesburg Mad Stone had been applied at least 130 times. The Leesburg Mad Stone had, according to the story, "never been applied to anyone who afterward developed any symptoms of hydrophobia."

The origins of the Leesburg Mad Stone was legendary (and perhaps mythical) as well. It supposedly came to America from Scotland in 1776, and it had "religiously preserved as one of the most valuable relics of the age" by the Fred family.

The story was that the Leesburg Mad Stone was mentioned in Chapter Seven of Sir Walter Scott's epic novel from 1825, *The Talisman*. The chapter concerned itself with a Saracen physician who cured a soldier of the Crusader army, and the same treatment was accorded to King Richard the Lionhearted.

Scott wrote, "although charmed stones have been dismissed from the modern Pharmacopoeia, its virtues are still applied to for stopping blood, and in cases of canine madness."

A number of people thought the Leesburg Mad Stone's power was "merely of a superstitious nature." Others, however, believed the power of the Leesburg Mad Stone was a "scientific reality."

One person who believed with certainty that the Leesburg Mad Stone worked was Luke E. Woodward of Winchester, Virginia. His late step-mother had been a member of the Fred family. She had, according to Woodard, inherited it from her father, and it had been in her family for generations before that.

Oddly, for a couple of generations, the Leesburg Mad Stone was worthless, because no one in the family knew how to clean it. Since it hadn't been cleaned correctly, it wouldn't adhere to wounds. Then, just by chance, an "old German" happened to spend the evening at the owner's home.

When told that the Leesburg Mad Stone wouldn't work because of lack of cleaning, the "old German" offered a the owner a deal. He said he'd show the owner how to clean it for half of it. The owner agreed to the deal, and a bargain was struck. Smiling, the "old German" said that the Leesburg Mad Stone could be easily placing it in warm water or warm milk.

The cleansing worked, and the "old German" took his half of the Leesburg Mad Stone with him back to Kentucky.

Woodard said that the Leesburg Mad Stone had failed only once. In that instance, the victim had waited for so long before seeking treatment that he already had symptoms when the stone was applied.

Woodard said that his step-mother had owned the Leesburg Mad Stone for many years, and that he had witnessed its "wonderful virtue" many times. He was more than willing to rattle off about any number of cases when the Leesburg Mad Stone successfully prevented hydrophobia.

On example of the Leesburg Mad Stone's virtue concerned the daughter of Rose Catts who lived at West End, Alexander, Virginia. She and a young man were bitten at the same time about 20 years before. Catts took his daughter to the Leesburg Mad Stone and it was applied. The girl had never shown any indication of developing rabies and was healthy in 1898.

The story of the young man bitten at the same time as Miss Catts wasn't a happy one. He didn't get any treatment and a few weeks later he died in great agony.

Another example relayed by Woodard was the case of Willie Dudley. Willie was the young son of F. E. Dudley, and the nephew of Judge H. M. Dudley. They all lived in Rappahannock County, Virginia. Willie received serious wounds on his face and head from a dog suspected of being rabid. The worst wound was near the boy's temple.

The boy's father carried him to Leesburg and received application of the Leesburg Mad Stone. It adhered to the boy's temple and even though the boy moved around in the bed, the

Mad Stone wouldn't be dislodged. It did finally fall of its own accord some 24 hours later.

After the Leesburg Mad Stone fell off, it was immersed in warm water for about 20 minutes, and when removed, the liquid was "full of greenish yellow scum."

The Leesburg Mad Stone "refused" to stick to any of the boy's other wounds and he was sent home. His wounds healed, and he never developed any symptoms of hydrophobia.

Another case was that of Mrs. J. H. Zirkle or Luray, Virginia. After a supposed mad dog snapped her, Zirkle came to Leesburg for treatment. The Leesburg Mad Stone wouldn't stick to any of her wounds, indicating that the rabies virus wasn't inside her body. This was confirmed when she never showed any signs of getting rabies.

Woodard conceded that some of the suspected mad dogs didn't actually have rabies. But he added quickly that it was "hardly likely" that all 130 cases involved healthy dogs. He then restated his belief that the Leesburg Mad Stone was effective in preventing hydrophobia.

1899

[Tennessee] March 20, 1899. There was a rampant rabies outbreak in Franklin and Coffee counties.

M. B. Christion was bitten by a mad dog near his home in Franklin County just south of Tullahoma. He immediately went to Summitville in Coffee County and had a Mad Stone applied to his wound. The Mad Stone adhered to the wound for two days before dropping off.

Feeling fine, Christion returned to his home.

A few days later, Laura Betty was walking down a street in Tullahoma when a dog suspected or rabies came after her. Betty used her umbrella and bravely fended off the canine. The dog tried several times to rip out her throat, but she battled it and it never got close enough to bite her.

[Tennessee] July 10, 1899. Sarah Mabe of Sparta, Tennessee was scratched on the temple by a cat. The cat scratch caused Mabe considerable discomfort, and she thought a Mad Stone might help.

Mabe went to the home of W. J. Winstead, and he applied his Mad Stone to her wound. It adhered to her injured temple for 23 hours, before it disengaged. Afterward, it wouldn't stick again.

As for the cat, it was watched, and after it had one fit after another, it was finally killed.

1900

[Tennessee] July 15, 1900. The seven-year-old son of Ike Wray, who lived near Alamo in Crockett County, was bitten by a mad dog. Wray took his child to Maury City near Humboldt, where Mrs. J. F. Russell applied her Mad Stone. After the treatment, the boy was believed to be free of the rabies virus, and the threat of hydrophobia was quickly forgotten.

Then, on the morning of December 11, a Dr. Cooke was called in to see the suddenly ill child. Cooke found the child in the deadly clutches of rabies. The child couldn't drink, "or even bear to look at water."

Cooke and several other physicians did their best, but it was a hopeless situation. After days of suffering, the child died on December 17.

[Kentucky] December 20, 1900. T. C. O'Bryan of Morton's Gap, Kentucky took his sons, Carl, and Elmore, to Henderson for a Mad Stone treatment. The boys had been bitten a few days before by a dog believed to be rabid.

The Mad Stone was owned by a doctor in Henderson. This particular Mad Stone was reputed to "possess rare virtue," Regardless of its reputation, O'Bryan said that if the Mad Stone didn't stick to his sons' wounds, he'd take them to the east, and that he'd have them treated by another Mad Stone.

Chapter Sources:

"Bitten by a Mad Dog." *The Nashville American*, April 19, 1896.

"Bitten by a Mad Dog." *The Nashville American*, August 12, 1896.

"Bitten by a Mad Dog." *The Nashville American*, January 6, 1898.

"Bitten by a Mad Dog." *The Nashville American*, June 4, 1896.

"Died of Hydrophobia." *The Nashville American*, December 18, 1900.

"Died of Hydrophobia." *The Nashville American*, July 21, 1896.

"Fought a Mad Dog." *The Nashville American*, July 5, 1898.

"Fought a Mad Dog." *The Nashville American*, July 9, 1898.

Gammon, CL. *The Fountain of Youth at Red Boiling Springs, Tennessee: Part 1*. Lafayette, Tennessee: Deep Read Press, 2024.

"Mad Dog Scare." *The Nashville American*, April 20, 1898.

"Madstone a Success." *The Nashville American*, April 6, 1899.

"Madstone." *The Nashville American*, December 7, 1896.

Scott, Sir Walter. *The Talisman*. (Several editions)

"Seeking a Madstone." *The Nashville American*, April 6, 1899.

"Seeking a Madstone." *The Nashville American*, December 21, 1900.

"Sparta Notes." *The Nashville American*, July 15, 1899.

"State." *The Nashville American*, November 16, 1897.

"Suit for Madstone." *The Nashville American*, November 12, 1898.

"Two Men Bitten." *The Nashville American*, June 18, 1897.

"Will Convene May 4." *The Nashville American*, May 2, 1897.

7. 1901-1905

1901

[Tennessee] March 24, 1901. Early in the morning, the 12-year-old son of George Allen of Liberty, DeKalb County, was bitten by a dog. The animal showed all the signs of having "highly developed" rabies.

The gravely injured boy's wounds were dressed, and then his father hurried with him to the town of Burt in Hickman County for a Mad Stone treatment. The stone adhered and stayed affixed to the wound for several hours before falling off.

Allen reported that the boy was improving.

[Tennessee] June 5, 1901. Tom Patterson Roberts was a well-known African American living in Pulaski. His wife was walking on Cornersville Pike on her way to "the Hurricane" community where her husband was cultivating a crop.

About a mile northeast of Pulaski, a dog owned by a tenant of the farm owned by Postmaster Peter Clark came upon the unsuspecting woman from behind. The dog's sharp teeth ripped at the woman's hand, gashing it open.

Mrs. Roberts went on to Pulaski and consulted with doctors Wilson and Butler. They cauterized the wound, and then they applied Major J. B. Stacey's Mad Stone to it. Stacey's Mad Stone was considered to be "one of the best in the section."

Due to her double treatment, Mrs. Roberts was expected to survive.

[Tennessee] July 13, 1901. An African American woman named Emma Howard from Elora in Lincoln County died from hydrophobia. She was bitten by a mad dog in April and received a treatment from a Mad Stone practitioner. The Mad Stone adhered "very strongly," and was believed to have accomplished its purpose.

Howard's wound healed, and the incident was all but forgotten until she became suddenly ill and died quickly.

[Tennessee] August 27, 1901. In Nashville, there was an effort to dispel the myth that Dog Days was the "regular season" of the year in which hundreds of mad dogs ran amok throughout communities, and that anyone bitten would develop rabies unless the dog was killed, and a Mad Stone was applied to his wound.

Those discounting treatments by the miracle rocks said a whetstone would have as much effect as a Mad Stone.

[New York] August 27, 1901. The validity of Mad Stones took a blow when it was found that most "rabies scares" were not based on reality. Dr. Wilcox of New York investigated 11 alleged deaths from mad dog bites. His investigation found that not one of the deaths was due to rabies.

In another case, Dr. Elmer Lee ended a rabies scare on Staten Island. He autopsied an alleged mad dog and determined it died from heart worms, not from rabies.

[Pennsylvania] August 27, 1901. Decades after the vaccine for rabies was developed, there remained skeptics in the medical community as to whether there was such a thing as hydrophobia. Some stated their belief that hydrophobia resulting from dog bites had "no existence except in the imagination." Many who wouldn't go that far, held that cases were not nearly as common as supposed. According to the medical professionals, the number of rabid dogs were not half as great as reported.

Of course, if the transmission of rabies was a myth, then the "marvelous stories of cures effected by Mad Stones" were a myth as well.

One of the skeptics was Dr. Matthew Woods. He was a leader among the members of the Philadelphia Medical Society. In one of his many dissertations on the subject of rabies he wrote that, "at the Philadelphia dog pound, where on an average more than 6,000 vagrant dogs are taken annually, and where the catchers and keepers are frequently bitten while handling them, not one case of hydrophobia has occurred during its entire history of twenty-five years, in which time 150,000 dogs have been handled."

Dr. Woods stated that the evidence supported the opinion that what was referred to as human rabies was the result of a "disordered imagination." In other words, fear. In animals, so held Dr. Woods, rabies was fundamentally due to mistreatment, or malnutrition, or both.

The following doctors endorsed Dr. Woods' opinion: Dr. Theophilus Parvin of Jefferson Medical College, and President of the National Academy of Medicine; Dr. Thomas G. Morten, Coroners Physician; Dr. Charles K. Mills of the University of Pennsylvania, and Dr. Thomas I. Mays of the Polyclinic Hospital.

Dr. Charles W. Dulles, a lecturer on the History of Medicine at the University of Pennsylvania, Consulting Surgeon to Rush Hospital and Manager of University Hospital, was also unsure about rabies. After his sixteen-year investigation of rabies on the behalf of the Pennsylvania Medical Societies, he wrote that he was "inclined to the view that there is no such specific malady." He continued that he had "failed to find a single case on record that can be conclusively proved to have resulted from the bite of a dog or any other cause."

Dr. Dulles, continued, "I might cite my own experience in the treatment of persons bitten by dogs supposed to be mad, which has furnished not a single case of the developed disease in thirty years. And I have probably seen more cases of so-called hydrophobia than any other medical man."

[National] August 27, 1901. Mad Stone "cures" began with misdiagnosing dogs as having rabies. In order to inform "those who dread hydrophobia, and whose fears are aroused every time they see a dog acting in an unusual manner," The American Society for the Prevention of Cruelty to Animals felt the need to issue the following:

1. It is supposed that a mad dog dreads water. It is not so. The mad dog is very likely to plunge his head to the eyes in water, though he cannot swallow it, and laps it with difficulty.
2. It is supposed that the mad dog runs about with evidences of intense excitement. It is not so. The mad dog never runs about in agitation; he never gallops; he is always alone, usually in a strange place, where he jogs alone slowly. If he is approached by a dog or man, he shows no sign of excitement, but when the dog or man is near enough, he snaps and resumes his solidary trot.
3. If a dog barks, yelps, whines, or growls, that dog is not mad. The only sound a mad dog is known to emit is a hoarse howl, and that but seldom. Even blows will not extort an outcry from a mad dog. Therefore, if any dog, under any circumstance, utters any other sound than that of a hoarse howl, that dog is not mad.
4. It is supposed that the mad dog froths at the mouth. It is not so. If a dog's jaws are covered or flecked with a white froth, that dog is not mad. The surest of all signs that a dog is mad is a thick and ropy brown mucus clinging to his lips, which he often tries vainly to tear away with his paws or to wash away with water.

[New Mexico Territory] December 15, 1901. Even after the turn of the century, the Old West was still the Old West. Cowboys still rode the open range and they still spent time in the "High

Lonesome." Of course, western cattle towns were much like towns everywhere else. That included the fact that large numbers of stray dogs roamed the streets.

A man in a cattle town in New Mexico Territory was bitten by a dog suspected of having rabies. A local doctor treated the man, but the man's arm still became extremely swollen, and a "thin bule streak" ran to his elbow. The blue streak was thought to indicate the course of the rabies virus.

Word went out and a Mad Stone was delivered to the injured man "from a distance." It isn't certain that the man purchased the Mad Stone, but in 1901, the average price paid for a Mad Stone was about $500.

The Mad Stone was applied to the wounded man's arm, and it adhered at once. It supposedly drew out the poison, as evidenced by the fact that the blue streak gradually diminished until it was gone, and the Mad Stone fell off.

After the treatment, the Mad Stone was immersed in water, and a blue film formed on the surface immediately.

For cowboys who spent their nights sleeping under a blanket of stars, the fear of mad dogs wasn't as great as their fear of rabid skunks. Since they were usually bitten while fully clothed and sleeping on the ground, most cowboys were bitten in the face.

Cowboys bitten by a rabid animal thought that since the nearest doctor was 20 to 50 miles away, their only hope rested with a Mad Stone treatment. They would seek one franticly, and they held on with ironclad faith that the Mad Stone would work. They had to have faith. They had nothing else.

[North Carolina and Virginia] December 15, 1901. A mad dog bit H. P. Morgan of Manchester, Virginia. On December 17, he headed out to North Carolina in search of a Mad Stone. Morgan's story follows:

"When I left here, I was almost on the verge of insanity, whether from the effect of the bite or the horrible mental strain I had been in since the occurrence, I know not, but I felt as though I'd go mad.

"On Thursday (December 20) at about noon the stone was applied. It was a small flat stone about the size of a half dollar, and when it was placed on the wound, immediately held fast, there was no shaking it off. So, it remained for 138 hours, at the expiration of which time having absorbed all the poison in the wound, it dropped off." Morgan related that the procedure was virtually painless.

He brought a small Mad Stone home with him and he applied it to his wound several times, but it wouldn't adhere, proving to him that he was free of the virus.

1902

[Tennessee] May 12, 1902. The nine-year-old daughter of Ral Houls of Sequatchie in Marion County was bitten on the arm by the family pet.

Houls did not kill the dog. Instead, he chained it up and was having it watched closely for signs of hydrophobia. The dog continued to snarl and snap which was more likely to its circumstances than to its having rabies.

Fearing the dog might be rabid, On May 16, Houls brought the girl to South Pittsburgh to have a Mad Stone applied.

The Mad Stone belonged to a Dr. Mitchell. It had been in his family, so went the story, for generations. It was sent to his grandfather by a member of a different branch of the Mitchell family who was moving to Texas.

Despite the length of time his family had owned it, this was the first time that Mitchell had ever applied the Mad Stone. When he placed it on the girl's injured arm, the Mad Stone adhered immediately, and it remained attached for two hours. The next day, the Mad Stone was placed on the girl's wound again. The plan was to repeat treatments daily for as long as the Mad Stone adhered.

[Tennessee] May 24, 1902. Tommy McNeely, the four-year-old son of Nick McNeely of Kenton, was bitten during the evening by a strange dog.

Fearing their son had been bitten by a rabid animal, the boy's parents were nearly in a state of panic. Nick McNeely telephoned Union City and inquired about a Mad Stone he had heard was there. He was told that a man at Woodland Mills had a Mad Stone and that he had used it to cure many people. Relieved, McNeely said he'd bring the boy to Woodland Mills for treatment as quickly as possible.

[Kentucky and Tennessee] December 1, 1902. W. H. Howard came to State Line, Kentucky from his home in Milan, Tennessee. He believed he had been bitten by a mad dog, and he desired a treatment from a Mad Stone.

L. D. Maddox applied his Mad Stone to Howard's wound, but it wouldn't adhere. A happy man, Howard was sure that he wouldn't develop hydrophobia.

1903

[Kentucky] February 11, 1903. J. W. Armstrong, age 13, of Christian County, Kentucky was taken to Paducah for a Mad Stone treatment. Armstrong was bitten on the right hand several days before by a dog suspected of having rabies.

Those fearing they had been bitten by mad dogs often came to Paducah to take advantage of the famous Mad Stone owned by Captain J. W. Fowler. On this occasion, Captain Fowler applied the Mad Stone and it stuck to the boy's wound for five hours before releasing itself.

The teenager returned home certain that he would not "come down" with hydrophobia.

[Tennessee] April 7, 1903. A dog thought to be rabid ran amok in Clay County, near Celina, Tennessee. The dog bit several dogs, and a number of cows and other livestock. Worse than the animals bitten, the dog left teeth marks in two of the children of James "Jim" Davis, before his wife shot and killed it.

A Mad Stone was applied to the children, and it was supposed that it had the desired effect. Davis happily reported that the boys were "all right."

Sadly, Davis was mistaken about one of his kids. Little Jeff D. Davis, age 3, was far from "all right." On the morning of April 23, proving positively that the Mad Stone treatment had failed, Jeff D. died "in terrible agony; with all the symptoms of hydrophobia."

The good news was that the other Davis child was healing quickly and he displayed no symptoms of rabies.

[Tennessee] May 6, 1903. A suspected mad dog bit two boys, some cows, and other livestock at Estill Springs in Franklin County. The dog was killed, and the livestock were herded into pens and watched to see if they exhibited signs of rabies.

Early the next morning, the boys were sent nearby to receive a Mad Stone treatment. The hope was that "nothing of a serious nature" would arise from their dog bites.

[Indiana and Ohio] May 7, 1903. Lura Ann Silcox of Attica, Ohio came to New Castle, Indiana and had the famous "Bundy Mad Stone" applied to her hand. She had been by a dog suspected of having rabies in January.

The swelling in her hand moved to her arm. Her arm was so swollen that her doctors recommended that it be amputated. Instead of giving up her arm, Silcox chose to have the Bundy Mad Stone applied.

After 180 hours the Mad Stone had still not fallen off Silcox's arm on its own. It was the second longest time the Bundy Mad Stone had ever remained adhered to a dog bite. When the Mad

Stone was full, it was dipped in milk for a few minutes to allow the poison to ooze out, then it was reapplied.

The Mad Stone owner, Henry Bundy, said that hundreds of others had been cured, and he expected Silcox to return to Ohio cured.

[Kentucky] June 15, 1903. The wife of well-to-do Bowling Green, Kentucky farmer, Will Rogers, returned home after Mad Stone treatment. She was said to be "entirely recovered."

A few days earlier, Mrs. Rogers was bitten on the lip by a family pet. The dog, a small feist, had never been ferocious before. However, soon after it bit Mrs. Rogers, it became "very wild, and had to be killed."

Mrs. Rogers became ill soon after receiving the bite, and "for some time her life was despaired of." She was taken to Rocky Hill, Edmondson County, Kentucky where she received a Mad Stone application. The Mad Stone adhered to her lip six consecutive times. She felt better almost immediately, upon treatment, and she was able to return home free of pain and apprehension.

The practitioner had been applying Mad Stones for more than a decade and he had reputedly saved many lives.

[Mississippi] June 20, 1903. John Brooks, a wealthy planter in Marshall County, Mississippi died of hydrophobia.

In the early May, during a rampage, a suspected mad dog bit Brooks and 12 others. All 13 received Mad Stone treatments.

Brooks showed absolutely no symptoms until July 17 when he became suddenly ill. His condition worsened steadily, and after three days of excruciating pain, he died.

None of the other bit victims experienced any symptoms of hydrophobia.

[Kentucky] June 29, 1903. A cat was acting "strangely" around the home of Albert Atkins near Linton, Trigg County, Kentucky. The cat finally ran under the house and it could be heard "growling."

Worried that the cat might be a threat, Mrs. Atkins decided to do something about it. She lifted a flood plank, and then she peered into the blackness using an oil lamp to get as much light as possible.

Before Atkins could locate the cat, it bounded through the floor opening and with its powerful jaws, and sharp teeth, chomped down on the woman's hand with a death grip. The feline held on so strongly that it had to be killed to get it off the poor woman's hand.

Mrs. Atkins had a Mad Stone applied to her deep wound, and it adhered on seven occasions. The practitioner promised Atkins that the poison had been extracted and that she was safe. She then returned home to recover.

[Kentucky and Tennessee] July 12, 1903. The previously mentioned L. D. Maddox of State Line, Kentucky remained in demand for his skill with a Mad Stone. He even took his Mad Stone on the road sometimes.

A number of people had been bitten by a suspected mad dog in Dresden, Tennessee recently. Maddox went there to treat an entire family that had been bitten. Maddox was confident of success. He said that there had never been a known case of rabies developing in any of his patients after he applied his Mad Stone.

[Kentucky] August 1, 1903. Mrs. David Woods returned to her home near Cerulean Springs, Trigg County, Kentucky. She had been in Paducah receiving a Mad Stone treatment for a dog bite just above the ankle on one of her legs. The dog that bit Woods wasn't believed to be rabid, but her suffering was intense, and the hope was that a Mad Stone would lessen it.

When the Mad Stone was applied, it adhered to the wound for several hours and had the desired effect of reducing the woman's pain and anxiety.

[Ohio] August 2, 1903. Most American states never officially condoned the use of Mad Stones, but the state of Ohio did for at least nine years, or so it appeared.

On August 2, a Mrs. Waugh of Columbus, Ohio went to the relic room of the statehouse there. She said she had been bitten by a mad dog and asked for the Mad Stone kept there to be applied to her wound. The curator of the museum obliged Mrs. Waugh and applied the state-owned Mad Stone.

The dog turned out to be free of rabies, but Waugh soon became critically ill. She was diagnosed with blood poisoning, and the presumption was that she contracted it from the Mad Stone.

The Waugh case prompted several doctors already opposed to the Mad Stone to renew their "agitation in favor of stopping its use." These doctors denounced Mad Stone use to cure or prevent rabies as utter "humbug."

The Mad Stone applied in the Waugh case was previously owned by an African American Civil War veteran named Aurelius Depp from Powell, Delaware County, Ohio. When Depp died in 1894, he bequeathed the Mad Stone to the State of Ohio, and it had been in the museum at the statehouse ever since.

The Mad Stone was not a mere curiosity, for school children on field trips to marvel at in amazement; it was put to use. While in the state's custody, the Mad Stone had been applied scores of times to prevent the onset of hydrophobia.

The museum curator had always acted as the Mad Stone practitioner, and he had an established method of use. He boiled the Mad Stone in milk, and then he applied it to the open wound. If the Mad Stone adhered to the wound, it was presumed as evidence that the rabies virus was present. In that case, the Mad Stone was allowed to remain attached until it "released itself."

If the Mad Stone didn't adhere, then it was taken as proof positive that the patient was free of rabies. In that case, the supposed healthy patient was sent home and no other treatment of any kind was recommended.

The state of Ohio didn't actually oversee the Mad Stone's application, but it did maintain the Mad Stone, and it permitted its use. The doctors wishing to ban Mad Stone use claimed that by its tacit approval the Ohio government was an active participant in the humbuggery. They continued that the state was ultimately responsible for the damage the Mad Stone caused. They made the difficult to refute claim that not only did the Mad Stone do no good, but it could, as was shown in the Waugh case, actually cause harm.

But the physicians contended that the worst danger from the Mad Stone was that it gave patients a false sense of well-being, and it prevented them from seeking "rational treatment before it's too late."

Dr. Charles Oliver Probst, head of the Ohio State Board of Health, chimed in on August 15. He said that boiling the Mad Stone was a wise precaution because the boiling process would aid in preventing blood poisoning. If the Mad Stone weren't boiled, it would be dangerous to place it against a "raw wound." However, Probst cautioned against putting a hot Mad Stone against a wound. He said the hot Mad Stone would break down the tissues and make the wound vulnerable to poisoning from other sources.

Probst said there was no reason to rush to get a Mad Stone treatment. He pointed out that the Board of Health's laboratory could determine whether an animal was rabid or not in a few days.

[Kentucky] August 18, 1903. Jesse Harrell of Grayson County, Kentucky came to Bowling Green to have a Mad Stone applied to a bite wound on his arm made by a suspected rabid dog. The stone was applied to the wound, and the swelling in

Harrell's arm "vanished" immediately. By the next morning, Harrell appeared "entirely well."

The Mad Stone used to treat Harrell was owned by an elderly African American woman. It had a reputation of producing "many wonderful cures."

[Tennessee] November 1, 1903. A mad dog bit the infant son of Reverend William Tabor of Overton County. The child, Wheeler Reece Tabor, had one of his legs "badly lacerated and torn."

Tabor brought Wheeler to Crossville and a Mad Stone was applied. The Mad Stone attached to the wound and continued to grip it for 90 minutes before releasing. A second attempt was made later, but the Mad Stone refused to adhere.

[Tennessee] December 21, 1903. Two little boys were bitten by what was feared to be a rabid cat. One of the boys was James Pinckney McDonald Jr., age 8. He was son of Dr. James Pinckney McDonald Sr. The other boy was Raby Bryant Shearin, age 11. He was the son of George Washington Shearin, Sr.

The youngsters were suffering greatly. Their parents were alarmed and they thought the best course was to get the youngsters treated by a Mad Stone. The boys were taken from Shelbyville to Coffee County for Mad Stone treatments.

Both children lived to adulthood, and both served in the American military. McDonald rose to the rank of Colonel, and Shearin was a Private.

1904

[Tennessee] March 29, 1904. A mad dog showed up in Cannon County and went to the home of Howard Kittrell about two miles from Woodbury. The dog "excited suspicion by its strange behavior."

Kittrell, a well-to-do farmer, finally pulled his pistol and fired it twice. Both rounds struck the dog, but it didn't die immediately. Instead, "the dog grabbed the pistol with its mouth, wrenching it from Kittrell and biting man's hand and arm. The wounds the dog caused were severe.

At the prompting of his friends, Kittrell sought out a Mad Stone and had it applied to his wounds. Additionally, he planned a trip to Chicago to consult with a specialist.

1905

[Tennessee] September 21. 1905. Mad Stones continued to be considered valuable commodities. J. D. Hamilton of Nashville was selling his. Hamilton contended that his Mad Stone was one of the best in Tennessee. He was offering the Mad Stone for $300.

Hamilton still had the Mad Stone for sale on October 14.

[Tennessee] October 15, 1905. A mad cat bit two of Mr. and Mrs. James Russell children in Columbia. The parents were concerned and they planned to take their children for Mad Stone treatments.

Chapter Sources:

"Applied Madstone." *The Nashville American*, June 6, 1901.

"Bitten by a Dog." *The Nashville American*, August 1, 1903.

"Bitten by a Mad Dog." *The Nashville American*, November 3, 1903.

"Bitten by Rabid Dog." *The Nashville American*, March 27, 1901.

"Children at Columbia Bitten by a Mad Cat." *The Nashville American*, October 17, 1905.

"Cured by a Mad Stone." *The Nashville American*, August 20, 1903.

"Cured by a Mad Stone." *The Nashville American*, June 17, 1903.

"Death in Madstones." *The Nashville American*, August 16, 1903.

"Died of Hydrophobia." *The Nashville American*, April 25, 1903.

"Died of Hydrophobia." *The Nashville American*, July 18, 1901.

"Farmer Bitten by a Supposedly Mad Dog." *The Nashville American*, March 30, 1904.

"For Sale." *The Nashville American*, September 21, 1905.

"Kentucky Affairs." *The Nashville American*, February 21, 1903.

"Mad Cat." *The Nashville American*, June 30, 1903.

"Mad Dog at Celina." *The Nashville American*, April 11, 1903.

"Mad Dog." *The Nashville American*, May 8, 1903.

"Madstone Applied." *The Nashville American*, July 14, 1903.

"Madstone of No Avail." *The Nashville American*, June 19, 1903.

"Madstone Stuck Six Days." *The Nashville American*, January 1, 1901.

"Madstone Used." *Plymouth Tribune*, May 21, 1903.

"Madstone Wouldn't Stick." *The Nashville American*, December 3, 1902.

McBean, Eleanor. *The Poisoned Needle*. Mokelumne, California: Health Research, 1956.

"Rabies and Hydrophobia." *The Nashville American*, August 27, 1901.

"Sent to a Madstone." *The Nashville American*, December 23, 1903.

"South Pittsburgh." *The Nashville American*, May 18, 1902.

"The Madstone." *The Nashville American*, December 15, 1901.

"Will Try Madstone's Virtues." *The Nashville American*, May 26, 1902.

8. 1906-1910

1906

[Tennessee] September 1, 1906. The Hope Hill neighborhood of Humboldt, Tennessee was thrown into a panic by a suspected mad dog. The rampaging dog bit Addison Caldwell, Addie Killen, Addie's father, J. R. Killen, and an African American boy.

J. R. Killen was the last of the group to be bitten. He killed the vicious dog, but only after a "terrible struggle."

All the bite victims went to the home of Mrs. J. F. Russell at Maury City near Humboldt to receive treatment by her famous Mad Stone. However, before Addison Caldwell took his treatment, he received a telegram from his uncle, Dr. Ben Caldwell, instructing him to go directly to New Orleans and take the Pasteur rabies treatment. Caldwell followed his uncle's instructions. The other bite victims received the Mad Stone treatment, and Mrs. Russell stated that they were all free of rabies.

Mrs. Russell stated that her Mad Stone was the only one in the area. According to her, an old vagabond had pawned it to her husband in 1891, for $15. The man never returned, and Mr. Russell began using the Mad Stone.

Mrs. Russell stated the Mad Stone had had been used more than 100 times and only once had a patient died from rabies. That case was, according to her, an "indirect" death because the person died about six months after being bitten. She continued that in that in the sole instance of the Mad Stone's failure it couldn't be applied correctly because the patient was covered with sores and "his blood was in very bad condition."

Mrs. Russell was referring to the previously mentioned case of seven-year-old Wray boy. The little boy received a Mad Stone treatment and was declared free of rabies in July 1900. He then died from hydrophobia that December.

1907

[Tennessee] February 5, 1907. Clarence Cato, who lived near the Smith County community of Rome, was bitten by a greyhound. The dog was suspected to be rabid.

Cato immediately went on a search for a Mad Stone. He located one owned by a Mrs. Atwood. She lived near the Smith County community of Grant.

Atwood applied the Mad Stone and it adhered to Cato's wounds for several hours.

[Kentucky] March 17, 1907. A young man named Smith from Piney Camp Ground in Crittenden County, Kentucky was bitten by a mad dog in Marion. The dog that bit Smith was just one of many mad dogs running wild in the vicinity of Marion.

The number of suspected mad dogs around Marion remained a problem. This enticed shotgun wielding bands of men to comb the area, and they killed every stray dog they found.

When bitten, Smith started at once for Paducah to get a Mad Stone applied.

[Kentucky and Tennessee] March 19, 1907. J. B. Pate's 15-year-old son was bitten by a mad dog near Dresden, Tennessee. Pate took his son to State Lane, Kentucky on March 20 to receive the treatment from the famous Mad Stone there.

[Tennessee] March 24, 1907. There were said to be at least three Mad Stones in Giles County. One of them was owned by Irwin M. Smith.

Smith had decided he wanted a Mad Stone a few years before. His wife had been bitten by a copperhead snake, and her arm became badly swollen. Smith mounted his horse and rode to the house of his wife's cousin, Solomon Simmons. Simmons had a Mad Stone and Smith borrowed it.

While awaiting the Mad Stone to come, Mrs. Smith was given a pint of whiskey. Although she drank it down, the whiskey didn't relieve her excruciating pain.

When the Mad Stone was applied to the fang wounds, Mrs. Smith's pain vanished, and her arm swelling decreased quickly. The stone adhered for seven hours before Smith was satisfied that all the venom was gone.

After that day, Smith had always had a Mad Stone available.

[National] March 24, 1907. Supporters conceded that "considerable superstition clusters around both hydrophobia and Mad Stones." However, the denied that they were a "figment of the brain" or pure superstition.

They readily admitted that the history of Mad Stones and where they came from was cloudy. However, they all agreed that Mad Stones were effective treating dog bites, snake bites, spider bites, and insect stings.

[National] March 26, 1907., The American medical community was still "at variance" as to whether hydrophobia, if it even existed, could be cured by a Mad Stone. Some doctors, perhaps a large majority, felt the Mad Stone was a ridiculous superstition. But other doctors, as evidenced in this book, not only approved of their use, but they applied Mad Stones themselves.

[Kentucky] March 27, 1907. Jennie Pierce of Glasgow was believed to own the only "genuine" Mad Stone in that part of Kentucky. Called the "Edmunds Mad Stone," Pierce's famous Mad Stone had once belonged to Ed Edmunds.

Over the past 25 or 30 years, so went the story, the Mad Stone had been applied to 478 people who had been bitten by rabid dogs, cats, livestock, and other animals. Pierce said the Mad Stone had succeeded to cure every patient whose wounds had not healed.

The Mad Stone had been handed down from generation to generation, and Pierce considered it priceless.

[Tennessee] May 18, 1907. One of the leading doubters of Mad Stones in Tennessee said that if one "had faith in things magical," a toothpick would work as well as a Mad Stone.

[National] May 26, 1907. A number of doctors agreed with the supposition that Mad Stones could be useful, after a fashion. The journal *Medical Brief* carried an article stating that "these stones are of value, but they would be of more value if their limitations were understood."

The author admitted that Mad Stones weren't made of any "particular variety of stone or substance." He thought most Mad Stones were either calcareous or of a stoney formation. He said he had seen many of them, and no two of them were of the same "composition geologically considered." He continued that Mad Stones were "concentrations either vesical, renal, or biliary, and were found in the bladder, kidney, or liver of animals," especially deer. However, their exact composition wasn't really important, so held the doctor.

The writer stated that the primary value of Mad Stones were that they acted on the "same principle as a blotting paper did when absorbing ink." The only thing a Mad Stone needed to cure the patient was for it to be porous enough to have good absorbent and adhesive qualities. "Nothing mysterious about it," he wrote.

The Mad Stone's absorbent qualities would draw saliva from the mad dog, or venom from other animals which would prevent the saliva or venom from entering the victim's body.

The author discounted the alleged magical qualities of Mad Stones. He said they would stick if moisture was present, not just when the rabies virus was in the wound.

[Tennessee] June 30, 1907. Buck Evans and Irion Duffy were petting Evans' favorite cat when it bit them both. It was later believed that a mad dog had bitten the cat sometime earlier.

Mrs. J. F. Russell, of Maury City near Humboldt, was one of the most trusted Mad Stone practitioners in Tennessee. She treated both Evans and Duffy.

[Tennessee] July 4, 1907. Hershel White, age 10, the son of Mr. and Mrs. George White, was bitten by a dog near Trenton.

The incident took place in the morning, and fearing the dog was rabid, Hershel's parents took him immediately to be treated by Mrs. J. F. Russell. The busy Mad Stone applicator placed the famous Mad Stone on the boy's wounds.

Despite what they said, many Mad Stone practitioners were motivated by more than their desire to save lives. Several of them made good money for their services. Beyond any travel expenses they might incur, in 1907, the going rate was $5 per Mad Stone application, and an additional $3 for each hour the Mad Stone remained adhered to the wound. Since sometimes a Mad Stone might stick to a wound for more than 100 hours, treatments could cost the equivalent of two years' pay.

The excessive cost of the dubious treatments led to the belief that Mad Stone practitioners were charlatans. Many people placed Mad Stone applicators in the same class as of snake oil salesmen, and rain makers.

[Indiana] September 17, 1907. News from New Castle, Indiana was that Henry Bundy had died five days before his 82nd birthday. He had gained fame "as the owner of the celebrated Bundy Mad Stone which has brought hundreds of persons afflicted with various forms of infection to New Castle for treatment."

Bundy had valued his Mad Stone so much that he either kept it with him, or in his safety deposit box.

[Tennessee] October 1, 1907. A suspected mad dog had been running loose in Trousdale County. Before being killed, the dog bit three people, and several cows. The situation for those bitten was characterized as "very serious."

One of the bit victims was a little boy from Hartsville. The boy's uncle, Link Suddath, who was a fireman for the Louisville & Nashville Railroad, began a search for someone with a Mad Stone, but he didn't locate anyone quickly.

[Tennessee] October 14, 1907. Mrs. W. W. Rayburn of 173 Fain Street in Nashville brought her seven-year-old son to Dr. Levin Dickson Wright at Dickson for Mad Stone treatment.

Rayburn said that a "strange dog" had attacked and bitten her son outside her home. The dog "inflicted a number of ugly wounds" on the boy's leg. Mrs. Rayburn killed the dog and sent it to Vanderbilt University where it was tested for rabies by an analytical chemist. The tests proved the dog was in fact rabid.

Dr. Wright applied his Mad Stone and it adhered to the boy's wounds "tenaciously" when it was first applied. But it gradually relaxed its hold until it finally disengaged. Dr. Wright expressed confidence that his treatment had "furnished a safe and effective antidote" to the child's wounds.

Dr. Wright's Mad Stone reportedly came from the East Indies. It had been handed down from generation to generation, and it had been applied "many hundreds of times." According to Wright, he had personally applied his Mad Stone more than 90 times, and some of his patients had been bitten by "raving mad" dogs. Wright swore that none of his patients had ever "developed the least symptom of hydrophobia."

1908

[Kentucky] January 25, 1908. Mayor Charles R. Baugh, of London, Kentucky owned a Mad Stone. His Mad Stone had been taken from the "vitals" of a deer, and it looked somewhat different than most others described here. It was ivory colored, was a cube of about one inch, and was extremely porous.

The Mad Stone had once been much larger, but before he died, the original owner had cut the stone into several pieces and passed the pieces to his sons.

The Baugh Mad Stone had originally belonged to William Baugh who was born near Petersburgh, Virginia in 1765. He was the great-grandfather of Charles R. Baugh. William Baugh gave one piece of the Mad Stone to Charles R. Baugh's father, Abraham Baugh.

Charles R. Baugh felt his Mad Stone was so valuable that the only time he didn't have it on his person, it was in his safety deposit box. Because the Mad Stone was so precious to him, Baugh made patients come to his residence, and he applied it himself.

The story went that the Baugh Mad Stone had been applied successfully many times. Despite that, Baugh would not say for certain that it was a cure for hydrophobia, but he had no doubt that "hundreds, bitten and terror-stricken" people had "applied the stone, and went their way, confident of cure."

[Kentucky] February 7, 1908. At Mt. Herman, Monroe County, Kentucky, a presumed mad dog was on the loose. It bit little eight-year-old Willie Oliver on the arm. The next day, the boy's father, Fayette Oliver, carried him to Barren County to have the famous Edmunds Mad Stone applied.

[National] April 25, 1908. Amid growing calls for federal action on the subject, the Department of Agriculture's Bureau of Animal Industry issued a long report called *Rabies and its Increasing Prevalence*. The report sought to, among other things, dampen the belief that Mad Stones were an effective rabies preventative. The report stated:

"The public has a false sense of security from madstones, and their use is to distinctly to be discouraged." The report continued, "People have made long journeys and paid large sums for them. However, the value was no greater than a piece of blotting paper applied in the same way."

Bureau scientists had studied several Mad Stones, including one sent to it in which its owner claimed, "had prevented several cases of rabies." The studies indicated that some Mad Stones were nothing more than hairballs that came from the stomachs of wild or domestic animals. The consisted of "matted hair which the animal had licked from its body and swallowed."

However, the majority of Mad Stones, according to the report, were "masses of vegetable fibers such as clover and grain, which have gradually collected over a considerable period of time and are formed into a spherical shape by the contraction of the gastric walls."

Moreover, gallstones, calculi, and "in fact, any porous stones" could be used as Mad Stones, so went the report.

The report explained why Mad Stones adhered to wounds. Whether a Mad Stone stuck or not depended "entirely upon the amount of hemorrhage or discharge from the wound." Where the bleeding was "profuse, the blood infiltrates the meshes of the madstone, soon coagulates and tends to hold it in place, and it adheres for a considerable time ... Where the wound is small and the bleeding light, there is nothing to hold the stone in place, and it doesn't adhere."

[Alabama] May 19, 1908. John Adkins of Merrimack, Alabama, came to Huntsville for a Mad Stone treatment. He had sustained a dog bite wound to one arm.

A Dr. Haden was in charge of the treatment. The doctor boiled his Mad Stone in water for 20 minutes, then he placed it in milk until it was almost cool, and then he put the Mad Stone against the boy's arm. The Mad Stone adhered for 45 minutes, then it was cleaned, cooled, and replaced. The second time it stuck for another 30 minutes.

The Mad Stone was brought to America from England by Mary Bullard's great grandfather, and it had been "treasured" by the family for many years.

[Kentucky] July 8, 1908. Polly Reneau, a well-to-do woman from the Monroe County, Kentucky town of Fountain Run, came to Barren County to have the famous Edmunds Mad Stone applied. She had been bitten by a dog she feared was rabid. The application was declared to be a success.

Jennie Pierce stated that Reneau was the 498th person to be treated by the fabulous Edmunds Mad Stone. The majority of recipients, according to Pierce, had resided in either Kentucky or Tennessee.

[Alabama] July 19, 1908. R. H. Narmore, of Tuscumbia, Alabama shot and killed one of his dogs he suspected it of being rabid. However, the dog bit Narmore's little son, Neal before it was killed. The dog also bit a horse, a calf, and killed several chickens.

A Mad Stone was applied to Neal, and it was believed to have cured him.

[Kentucky] December 18, 1908. Wayne Dorsey, of Motely, Warren County, Kentucky, was the sone of Reno Dorsey. Wayne suffered a bite from a suspected mad dog, and Reno took him to nearby Barren County to have the renowned Edmunds Mad Stone applied. Jennie Pierce applied the Mad Stone four times before she was satisfied that all the mad dog virus was out of the boy's body.

Pierce informed those interested that Dorsey's treatment marked the 499th time that the remarkable Mad Stone had been applied.

1909

[Tennessee] May 13, 1909. In Lawrenceburg, D. C. Hill's long-time family dog became suddenly vicious. The old dog bit Hill's eight-year-old son, Willie, on the calf. The ugly wound was an inch and a half long, and an inch deep. The dog put up quite a battle, but the elder Hill was able to finally kill it.

There was no concern about little Willie until May 16, when another of Hill's dogs began to have what was supposed to be "mad fits."

Very worried about Willie's survival, D. C. began searching for a Mad Stone. He found a Mrs. Arnold living in Lawrence County who had a Mad Stone. It was applied to Willie's wound and it adhered foe 23 hours and 15 minutes before falling off.

[Tennessee] November 18, 1909. Jimmy Fly, age 8, the son of Hardy Leigh Fly, was bitten by a dog at his home in Gibson County. The dog was "especially vicious," and it made an "ugly wound" on the boy's throat and chin.

Fly took the boy to Mrs. J. F. Russell's home. Mrs. Russell said it was "extremely unusual" for a dog to go mad in late November. But she applied the Mad Stone, and it adhered for 24 hours.

Not fully trusting the Mad Stone treatment, Fly carried the boy to Memphis for the 21-day Pasteur treatment. After the double treatment, Fly was confident that hydrophobia would never visit his family.

Sadly, neither the Mad Stone nor the Pasteur treatment could save the boy. The lad developed what was believed to be rabies, and he died on December 16.

Mrs. Russell, who had for years said she had only lost one patient to rabies, had to adjust her record. Or did she? There is doubt as to whether the boy died of hydrophobia or not. His death certificate stated that the boy died from tonsillitis.

1910

[Alabama] April 11, 1910. Near Monte Sano Mountain. Alabama, the nine-year-old son of William Brooks saved his dog from a mongrel's attack. The mongrel, considered rabid, bit the boy several times during the melee.

Brooks brought his son to Huntsville and had a Mad Stone applied to the boy's wounds. However, the Mad Stone refused to adhere.

[Tennessee] April 24, 1910. Controversy had always swirled around the Mad Stone. Regardless of one's opinion, the Mad Stone was always a source of great interest. The editors of *The Nashville American* wrote they would "take it as a favor if anyone who owns or knows anything about a genuine 'madstone' will write us about it."

[Tennessee] August 8, 1910. Dr. William Litterer was instructor of Pasteur work in the bacteriological department at Vanderbilt University. He opposed Mad Stones in the strongest way possible. Litterer called Mad Stones treatments "fake, pure and simple." He said that Mad Stones were nothing more than gallstones and that they did no good at all. He contended that the Pasteur treatment was the only effective preventative treatment for hydrophobia.

In fact, according to Dr. Litterer, Mad Stone applications had "in a number of cases resulted in giving hydrophobia to patients instead of curing them." He cited one case from Knoxville when a Mad Stone was applied to a person with rabies, and it was later applied to the face of an infant suffering from the bite of a dog that wasn't rabid. Hydrophobia "germs" were, according to the doctor, transferred to the infant and the child contracted hydrophobia.

Dr. Litterer's statements had no effect on the believers for a couple of reasons:

1. Dr. Litterer didn't name those involved in the case he cited, rendering it no more than the same kind of anecdotal evidence that opponents scoffed at when presented by Mad Stone applicators.
2. Dr. Litterer seemed to confirm that Mad Stones worked. If Mad Stones didn't draw away the rabies virus, how could they transfer it? At least, that was the question the believers asked.

[Michigan and Massachusetts] August 8, 1910. After many years of allowing Mad Stone use in their states, the legislatures of Michigan and Massachusetts made Mad Stone application a felony. The reason for outlawing Mad Stone treatments was that they provided "false security" and in fact, spread hydrophobia.

Chapter Sources:

"Bitten by a Mad Dog." *Nashville Tennessean*, July 6, 1907.

"Bitten by a Mad Dog." The *Nashville American*, July 21, 1908.

"Bitten by Mad Dog." *The Nashville American*, March 21, 1907.

"Bitten by Mad Dog." *The Nashville American*, February 12, 1907.

"Bitten by Mad Dog, Boy Dies." *Nashville Tennessean*, December 18, 1909.

"Bitten by Mad Dog." *The Nashville American*, September 5, 1906.

"Brief State News." *The Nashville American*, February 12, 1907.

Carden, Thomas. "Mad Stone Lore." *The Nashville American*, March 24, 1907.

"Dog Star in Sky: 'Dog Days'." *Nashville Tennessean*, August 8, 1910.

"Faith in Madstones." *Nashville Tennessean*, October 13, 1907.

Fly, Jimmy. Death Certificate, December 16, 1909.

"Hydrophobia is a Constant Menace." The *Nashville American*, April 26, 1908.

"Information Bureau." *The Nashville American*, April 24, 1910.

"Kentucky Madstone Works Many Cures." *The Nashville American*, March 27, 1907.

"Madstone Adhered More than 23 Hours." *Nashville Tennessean*, May 29, 1909.

"Mad Stone Applied." *Nashville Tennessean*, July 10, 1908.

"Madstone Applied." The *Nashville American*, May 21, 1908.

"Madstone Cherished as Family Heirloom." *Nashville Tennessean*, January 25, 1908.

"Madstone is Applied." *The Nashville American*, April 13, 1910.

"Mad Stone is Applied." The *Nashville American*, December 20, 1908.

"Madstones." *The Nashville American*, May 26, 1907.

"Nashville Boy Tries Madstone." *Nashville American*, October 15, 1907.

"Questions and Answers." *The Nashville American*, March 16, 1907.

"Questions and Answers." *The Nashville American*, May 18, 1907.

"Stone Applied to Wound." *Nashville Tennessean*, November 28, 1909.

"Three People by a Dog." *Nashville Tennessean*, October 2, 1907.

"To Try Mad Stone." The *Nashville American*, February 10, 1908.

9. After 1910

1911

[National] May 21, 1911. Several "scientists of great prominence" stated the even if the Mad Stone worked, it was unnecessary. They stated that the Pasteur treatment was also necessary. They held their view based on their opinion based on their "conservative estimate" that even if there was such a thing as rabies, less than "one person in 1,000 bitten by a dog is in any danger of rabies." They continued that "if such a disease exists it is only in the most isolated cases."

[Kansas] August 1, 1911. Dr. J. S. Crumbine, Secretary of the Kansas State Board of Health, requested that State Attorney General Dawson clamp down on Mad Stone use. Dawson agreed and threatened a Mad Stone owner in Hutchinson with arrest if he attempted to treat a boy who had been bitten there a few days before.

State authorities then ordered Reno County officials to send the boy to the state university hospital at Rosedale, so the child could receive the Pasteur treatment.

[Tennessee] October 26, 1911. Three-year-old Ruby Burch was attacked and mauled by a mad dog. She was the daughter of William Burch, prominent merchant in the Lawrence County town of Leoma. She was playing in the road in front of her house when she was attacked.

A Mad Stone was applied to Ruby's wounds and it stuck for several hours. However, the child developed hydrophobia, and after much suffering, she died on December 3.

1913

[Tennessee] March 6, 1913. A Nashvillian wanted to trade a "genuine Madstone with a history," as well as two Remington typewriters. In exchange, he wanted a "high-grade" watch, a gun, or a diamond.

[Alabama] July 19, 1913. Dr. P. B. Moss served as the Alabama State Bacteriologist, and he headed the Alabama State Pasteur Institute. Moss tried, as others had many times before, to explode the myth that Dog Days marked an increase in rabid dogs. He also repeated the old refrain that Mad Stones were of no value in treating hydrophobia.

1916

[Tennessee] January 6, 1916. A mad dog bit the young son of Henry County farmer Henry L. Vaughn. The dog also bit several other dogs and livestock before beginning killed.

Vaughn took the boy to Puryear, where a Mad Stone was applied.

1923

[Tennessee] January 25, 1923. Mad Stones represented an old way of doing things. Old ways die hard, and applying Mad Stones died hard. Mad Stones were still in use four decades after the Pasteur Treatment was introduced.

W. H. Redford, who lived near Nashville, was bitten by a mad dog on January 22. Redford learned that Dixie Wright of McEwen had a Mad Stone, and he went there for treatment. Dixie applied the Mad Stone Redford's wounds twice. On the first application, it adhered for 17 minutes. On the second application, it stuck for 12 minutes.

Chapter Sources:

"Boy Bitten by Mad Dog." *Nashville Tennessean and The Nashville American*, January 14, 1916.

Burch, Ruby. Death Certificate, December 3, 1911.

"Farmer Uses Mad Stone To Treat Bite of Dog." *Nashville Tennessean and The Nashville American*, January 28, 1923.

"For Exchange." *Nashville Tennessean and The Nashville American*, March 6, 1913.

"'Mad Dog' Seldom Mad, Claim Made." *Nashville Tennessean and The Nashville American*, May 21, 1911.

"Madstone Failed." *Nashville Tennessean and The Nashville American*, November 17, 1911.

"'Old Idea of Dog Days Exploded." *Nashville Tennessean and The Nashville American*, July 20, 1913.

"Prohibit Use of Madstone." *Nashville Tennessean and The Nashville American*, August 2, 1911.

10. Cures and Preventatives

Over many, many years all kinds of rabies "cures" were brought forward other than Mad Stones, and the Pasteur treatment. Some of them could actually help in some cases, many were dangerous or deadly, and some of the treatments were just silly.

Below are a few of the alleged cures, as well as some of the things done to avoid hydrophobia:

- A vapor bath was said to cure hydrophobia. It didn't
- Wearing heavy clothing was believed to either prevent the animal's teeth from getting to the flesh, or it would wipe the saliva from the animal's teeth and prevent it from entering the body even if the teeth did break the skin. It was an excellent idea. Keeping as much of the virus out of the body as possible could offer at least limited protection.
- Various seeds from trees in the South American rain forest were believed to prevent or treat hydrophobia.
- Pilocarpine, an extract of jaborandi, was believed to be an effective antidote to the rabies virus.
- A silly belief was that killing a dog before it became rabid would prevent those bitten by the dog from developing hydrophobia.
- Eating garlic was said to act as a prophylactic to hydrophobia. Garlic is still used to prevent or help control several conditions.
- Of course, muzzling dogs would certainly prevent bites. But there was no one to muzzle stray dogs, and stray dogs were the most dangerous.
- Another silly belief was that people had nothing to fear from rabid animals, except during Dog Days.

- The Hoang Nan (Strychnos malaccensis) plant contains powerful alkaloids like strychnine and, more to a larger degree, brucine. It was used as a rabies treatment.
- The belief among some was that only those dogs that curled their tails to the left could get rabies. Those people only kept "right-tailed" dogs.
- Amputation of the digit or limb where the bite occurred was a recommended treatment. Amputation after the virus had entered the body was useless.
- An alcohol bath was touted as a hydrophobia cure. It had no effect on the rabies virus.
- An injection of a large quantity of morphine, followed by an injection of castor oil was thought to cure one with rabies. It didn't.
- Applying iodine to the wound was believed to help. Although it could be toxic, iodine was used to treat many kinds of wounds for decades.
- Steeping datura stramonium (Jimsonweed) leaves in water, then drinking the fluid, was believed by some to be an antidote. However, it could be toxic.
- Calomel (mercurous chloride) pills were consumed. The pills were also used for yellow fever, but they are dangerous due to their mercury content.
- Cauterizing the wound (usually with a red-hot metal rod) was recommended by many doctors. Again, if the virus had already entered the victim's system, cauterizing the wound wouldn't help.
- Cutting away the entire area of the bite was also an accepted practice. As with several other "cures" cutting away the wound area was ineffective if the virus was already in the victim's system.
- Cutting out the "little white knots" that developed under the victim's tongue after he was bitten, then soaking the

victim in a tub of salt water occasionally over the next 24 hours was tried. First, the "white knots" were a myth. Secondly, salt water would do nothing to affect the rabies virus.
- There was a belief that cutting off a dog's tail would prevent it from getting rabies. Oddly, this myth was based on fact – sort of. Scientists learned early on that the rabies virus "settled" in the spine. The myth then emerged that since the dog's tail was at the bottom of the spine, cutting it off would prevent the virus from settling.
- Dipping a dog's nose in frigid water was said to prevent it from getting rabies.
- Drinking vinegar was common in suspected rabies cases. Again, vinegar was, and is, consumed for many conditions.
- Eating the root of the poke plant was tried to prevent rabies. All parts of the poke plant are toxic, but some people still eat the leaves after soaking and cooking them in boiling water.
- Copper filings were rubbed into the wound to prevent rabies. Copper was, and is, believed in some circles to prevent and cure several conditions.
- Some people ate the very toxic belladonna plant in order to cure hydrophobia.
- One could eat the herb called skullcap to prevent hydrophobia. While the skullcap plant isn't toxic per se, overuse can cause liver damage.
- Rubbing a salted pickle on the wound was another treatment. It is possible that the salt and vinegar used to pickle the cucumber was believed to treat rabies.
- Simply dousing the rabies victim in frigid water was thought to work against the virus. Why this belief developed is not certain.

- Some believed that the Spitz was the only breed of dog that could contract rabies and avoiding that breed would ensure that one would never become rabid. The origin of this myth isn't certain.
- Some doctors believed that hydrophobia was imaginary, and since it was psychosomatic, those that didn't believe in rabies were safe from the condition. There are still some who doubt that rabies is real.
- Some of the "hair of the dog that bit you" was a cure. One would take some of the mad dog's hair and either chew it, swallow it, or bind it on the wound. This old remedy is a head scratcher.
- Pulling out the rabies virus with a suction device was, for a time, an accepted medical practice. Sucking out the virus might be effective, to a degree, if action is taken very quickly. But simply washing the wound with soap and water would be as effective, or more so, than using a suction device.
- Swallowing strychnine was another remedy used. Strychnine is a deadly poison, but desperate times require desperate measures, and many people were willing to accept the risk.
- One method was to cut out the heart of a mad dog, boil it in water, then drink the broth it produced. This method, beyond being disgusting, might actually introduce rabies or other diseases into the patient's system.
- The belief among some was that African Americans were immune from the rabies virus; thus, they didn't need any remedy.
- The kiss of a king was said to cure rabies.
- There was a myth that extremely cold winters caused mad dog outbreaks during the following spring. Therefore, if

- the previous winter was mild, one need not be concerned with coming across rabid animals.
- Three treatments a day of "bruised" elecampane root boiled in "new" milk and then swallowed was another remedy. If taken in substantial amounts, elecampane root could be dangerous.
- Touching a piece of a king's garment was thought to work just as well as anything else in preventing hydrophobia.
- Another preventive was washing the wound in warm water and vinegar, then, when the wound dried, dropping a few drops muriatic acid on it. Muriatic acid causes severe burns, and it was used to produce a cauterizing effect. In truth, washing the wound might help, and the muriatic acid might have a limited effect, but the vinegar did nothing.
- For years, there was a general belief that only dogs could transmit rabies. People paid no attention to the bites of other animals. Later, cats and wild animals were included as agents of hydrophobia, but the focus remained on dog bites.
- Zinc-chloride applied to the wound was another preventative. Zinc-chloride produces toxic and corrosive fumes, and it can be absorbed into the body through the skin. It is extremely dangerous.

Chapter Sources:

"A Cure for Hydrophobia." *The Republican Banner*, June 23, 1872.

"Another Cure for Hydrophobia." *The Republican Banner*, September 21, 1873.

"A Woman Who Cures Hydrophobia." *Daily American*, July 27, 1876.

"Current Topics." *The Republican Banner*, July 8, 1868.

"Hydrophobia and its Prevention." *The Republican Banner*, June 21, 1872.

"Hydrophobia." *Daily American*, December 9, 1877.

"Left-Tailed Dog." *The Daily American*, April 29, 1879.

"Poke Root as an Antidote for Hydrophopia." *The Republican Banner*, March 17, 1869.

"___" *The Daily American*, April 22, 1885.

"___" *The Daily American*, January 14, 1884.

"___" *The Daily American*, June 23, 1881.

"___" *The Daily American*, September 21, 1887.

"The Dog." *The Daily American*, June 19, 1885.

"The Latest Hydrophobia Remedy." *Daily American*, November 21, 1877.

"___" *The Republican Banner*, November 12, 1872.

"The Torments of Hydrophobia." *Daily American*, August 4, 1877.

"White Bluff." *The Daily American*, June 11, 1880.

11. Ancient Mad Stones

While this book looks mainly at the Mad Stone phenomenon in Middle Tennessee, the belief and usage of Mad Stones was common throughout the United States and indeed the world. And while this book covers only about half a century, the application of Mad Stones was ancient in its origins and usage.

Stories of Mad Stone types of cures were common as far back as ancient Persia.

Greek historian, Pliny the Elder in his work *Natural History*, (published around the year 77 A.D.) stated that some stones from animals called "bezoars" acted as antidotes to poison.

Bezoar stones are the items from antiquity most often associated with the Mad Stones of America. Though the origin of bezoar stones was debated, (they were thought to come from the head, liver, or eyes of certain animals, or even deer tears), bezoars were believed to be effective against all kinds of poisons and were thought to be produced by animals as a self-defense against animal bites and poisonous plants.

An actual bezoar is a mass of hardened undigested material found in the digestive systems of deer, antelope, goats, oxen, and llamas. Stomach contractions squeeze and smooth it into a roughly round shape.

Believers in the powers of Mad Stones pointed to other historical references as proof of its validity. A myth arose that Sir Walter Scott's novel, *The Talisman,* mentioned a particular Mad Stone that was later brought to America and came to be called the Leesburg Mad Stone. However, there was no proven connection between Scott's story and the Leesburg Mad Stone.

There were many other mentions of Mad Stones.

Jean Baptist Tavernier in *Travels in India* from 1677 wrote, "I will finally make mention of the snakestone which is nearly the size of a doubloon, some of them being oval shape being thick in the middle and thin toward the edges. Indians say it is grown on the heads of certain snakes, but I should rather believe that it is the product of the priest of the idolators, who made them think so, and that this stone is the product of certain drugs. Whatever it may be, it has an excellent virtue in extracting the poison from wounds inflicted by poisonous animals."

In *Experiments* published in 1685, Francisco Redi described Mad Stones (or snakestones) as being found in the heads of cobras living on the Indian subcontinent. The stones adhered to wounds until the poison was completely absorbed. Then the stones were cleansed by steeping them in warm milk.

In 1891, George Fredrick Kunz, a gem specialist, asserted in *Science Magazine* that the Mad Stone, or snakestone, was actually a tabasheer. A tabasheer is a kind of opal "found in the joints of the bamboo" in the Indian subcontinent. This stone was formed when the bamboo juice dried and hardened into a solid. It had been mentioned as a treatment since before the 10th Century. When placed in the mouth, so went the story, it would stick to the palate. Additionally, it would cause water to "boil in a glass."

Sir David Brewster (1781-1868) said Mad Stones were found in the joints of diseased corn stalks and formed by hardening sap. He continued that it was also applied to treat fevers, colds, and biliousness (irritability and bad temper).

Some people contended that Mad Stones didn't come from animals at all. Instead, they were formed in the Silurian Period more than 400 million years ago along with several kinds of coral.

The above examples added weight to Mad Stone believers and provided them with ammunition against Mad Stone doubters.

About the Author

CL Gammon has had a life-long fascination with the written word. This fascination has led to his authoring more than 70 books.

Gammon, studied Political Science at Tennessee Technological University and History and Government at Hillsdale College

Over the years, Gammon has received several prestigious honors and awards. He has twice received the Certificate of Appreciation for Service to the State of Tennessee (2018 and 2025), the Partisan Prohibition Historical Society Citation of Merit (the only two-time recipient), and nomination for the 2023 Gilder Lehrman Lincoln Prize.

Several universities, including the State University of New York, the University of Akron, and East Mississippi Community College, have utilized his books as course material.

Articles written by Gammon have appeared in more than a dozen national and regional publications. He has also written feature articles for his hometown newspaper, *The Macon County Times*.

CL Gammon lives in Lafayette, Tennessee.

Index

Abernathy, Dr. Charles Clayton: 12, 20
Adams, John: 67-68
Adcock, W. H.: 53
Adkins, John: 101
Age, Silurian: 49, 117
Alabama: (Athens: 69); (Barbour County: 60); (Eufaula: 60); (Huntsville: 69, 101, 103); (Kendall: 63); (Lauderdale County: 63); (Merrimack: 101); (Monte Sano Mountain: 103) (Tuscumbia: 101)
Allen, George: 77
ASPCA: 80
Anderson, James: 60
Arizona: 18
Armstrong, J. W.: 83
Arnold, Mrs.: 102
Arnold, Welcome: 21
Arrington, Dr. D. L.: 58-59
Atkins, Albert: 86
Atwood, Mrs.: 94
Bader, C. H.: 38
Baker, Dr.: 22
Baker, John: 21
Bank, Loudoun National: 70
Barbiere, Joseph: 18
Baugh, Abraham: 99
Baugh, Charles R.: 99
Baugh, William: 99
Belcher, Mr.: 26
Berry, Mr.: 67
Betty, Laura: 73
Bezoar: 116
Biddle, Dr. W. M.: 41, 50
Blair, R. A.: 46
Booth, Dr.: 63
Borders, Mr.: 34
Bratton, Dr. Elijah: 27
Brooks, John: 85
Brooks, William: 103
Brown, James: 37
Brown, Sam: 64
Bryant, Mark: 30
Bullard, Mary: 101
Bumpus, Mr.: 32-33
Bunce, D. J.: 17-18
Bundy, Harry: 84-85, 98
Burch, Ruby: 107
Burch, William: 107
Bush, Dr.: 62
Butler, Dr.: 77
Butterfield, Jewett: 13
Caldwell, Addison: 93
Caldwell, Dr. Ben: 93
Calvin, DeWitt: 70
Carraway, Miss: 31, 63
Carter, B. F.: 11
Cato, Clarence: 94
Catts, Rose: 72
Cheatam, Lafayette: 44

Cherry, Dr.: 55
China: 22
Christion, M. B.: 73
Clark, Peter: 77
Clark, Watt G.: 35, 66
Cleveland, Mrs.: 58
Cloyd, W. S.: 19
College, Jefferson Medical: 79
Comley, Henry B.: 21
Cook, G. W. E.: 48
Cooke, Dr.: 74
Creek, Brush: 67
Creek, Carter's: 63
Creek, Dock: 64
Creek, Flat: 15
Creek, Haywood: 11
Creek, Richland: 11
Creek, Shipman's: 66
Creek, Whites: 53
Crumbine, Dr. J. S.: 107
Cummings, Officer: 68
Curtis, Bert: 44
Daily American: 45
Davis, James "Jim": 84
Davis, Jeff D.: 84
Dawson, Attorney General: 107
Days, Dog: 78, 108, 110
Demoville & Company, the: 69
Department of Agriculture, the: 100
Depp, Aurelius: 87
Dies, Robert: 26-27
Dinwiddie, Moses: 15

Dinwiddie. James Baugh: 15, 53
Dobbins, Daisey: 62
Dobbins, Tom M.: 62
Dorsey, Reno: 101
Dorsey, Wayne: 101-102
Driver, Monroe: 52
Dudderar, Samuel: 68
Dudley, F. E.: 72
Dudley, H. M.: 72
Dudley, Willie: 72
Duffy, Irion: 97
Dulles, Dr. Charles W.: 79
Dunmon, J. A.: 27-28
Elledge, Mr.: 24-25
England: 32, 101
Evans, Buck: 97
Evans, Turner: 17-18
Ewing, Dr. W. G.: 59
Fisher, Mack: 26
Fitzwilson, Mr.: 19
Fleming, Mr.: 17-18
Fletcher, Greenville: 23-24, 26-28
Florida, Pensacola: 24, 35
Floyd, Charles T.: 48
Fly, Hardy Leigh: 102
Fly, Jimmy: 102-103
Fowler, J. W.: 83
Franklin, Benjamin W.: 25
Franklin, Dr. William E.: 25
Fred, Mrs.: 70-71
Gandy, W. K.: 32
Gandy, Walter: 31

Georgia: (Banks County: 34); (Buena Vista: 43); (Cherokee County: 35); (Elbert County: 34); (Forsyth County: 34); (Gerber: 42); (Hancock County: 34); (Homer: 34); (Irwin County: 45); (Lookout Valley: 42); (Marion County: 43); (Sparta: 35); (Troupe County: 34)

German, Mrs.: 70-71

Gilmore, H. C.: 26

Goodpasture, Arthur: 27

Green, Willow: 35-36

Greer, Murray: 37

Gunn, Allen: 60

Haden, Dr.: 101

Hair, M.: 43

Hall, Mrs.: 11-12

Halloway, Young: 31

Hallowell, Dr.: 33

Ham, Jesse: 64

Hamilton, J. D.: 90

Hanks, Robert: 34

Harrell, Jesse: 88-89

Hayes, Bud: 20

Health, Ohio Board of: 88

Henley, Peter: 62

Henry, John: 37

Hill, D. C.: 102

Hill, Willie: 102

Hoagland, Mr.: 46-47

Holden, F. R.: 40-41

Hopkins, G. A.: 20

Hospital, Polyclinic: 79

Hospital, Rush: 79

Hospital, Kansas University: 107

Houls, Ral: 82

Howard, Emma: 78

Howard, W. H.: 83

Huey, Charles: 48

Hunton, Eppa, Jr.: 70

Hunton, Eppa, Sr.: 71

Illinois: (Carthage: 48); (Chicago: 90); (Denver: 46, 49); (Hancock County: 46-47); (Kellerville: 48); (Lacon: 48); (Meredosia: 48); (Paris: 24); (Piper City: 48); (St. Mary Township: 48)

Indiana: (New Castle: 84, 98); (Rush County: 41); (Terre Haute: 24-25, 41-42); (Warren County: 42)

Indies, East: 98

Indies, West: 53

Industry, Bureau of Animal: 100

Insect: 22, 95

Institute, American Pasteur: 30

Iowa: (Cedar County: 17); (Iowa City: 17); (Linn County: 17); (Mechanicsville: 17); (Paris: 17); (Waterloo: 21)

Isbell, W. J.: 54-55

Jepson, Dr. J. J.: 54-55

Johnsey, Alice: 63

Johnsey, Elisa: 63

Johnsey, R. A.: 62-63

Johnson, James: 15

Johnson, L. C.: 13

Jolly, Dr. W. H.: 62

Joseph, Alexander: 11, 40, 50, 54, 58, 60-61, 64

Joseph, Virginia: 51

Kansas: (Reno County: 107); (Rosedale: 107)

Kavanaugh, James: 21

Kentucky: (Barren County: 100-102); (Bowling Green: 31, 54, 85, 88); (Cerulean Springs: 86); (Christian County: 61, 83); (Crittenden County: 94); (Edmondson: 85); (Fountain Run: 101); (Glasgow: 96); (Grayson County: 88); (Henderson: 46, 74); (Lincoln County: 68); (Linton: 86); (London: 99); (Louisville: 13); (Madison County: 46-47); (Marion: 94); (Monroe County: 99, 101); (Morton's Gap: 74); (Motely: 101); (Mt. Herman: 99); (Mt. Sterling: 44); (Paducah: 83, 86, 94); (Pembroke: 61); (Piney Camp Ground: 94); (Portland: 13); (Pulaski County: 67); (Rocky Hill: 85); (Simpson County: 31); (Somerset: 67); (Stanford: 68); (State Line: 83, 86); (Trigg County: 86); (Warren County: 54, 101); (Webster County: 46)

Killen, Addie: 93

Killen, J. R.: 93

Kindred, Eugene: 62

King, Dr.: 55

King, Mr.: 26

Kirk, John: 41-42

Kitrell, Howard: 89

Kroger, Frederick: 21

Lampley, William: 64

Lee, Dr. Elmer: 78

Lincoln, Abraham: 9, 25

Lincoln, Robert Todd: 9, 25

Litterer, Dr. William: 103-104

Lockhart, Mr.: 34

Louisiana, New Orleans: 93

Lynn, Mrs. Wash: 35

Mabe, Sarah: 74

Mad Stone: (Arnold: 102); (Atwood: 94); (Baugh: 99); (Biddle: 41, 50); (Bratton 27); (Bumpus: 32-33); (Bundy: 84-85, 98); (Carraway: 31, 63); (Clark: 35, 66); (Dinwiddie: 15, 53); (Driver: 52);)(Dudderar: 68) (Edmunds: 96, 100-102); (Eufaula: 60); (Evans-Fleming: 17-18); (Flecther: 22-23, 26-28); (Fowler 83); (Fred: 70-71); (Haden: 101); (Hair: 43); (Hamilton: 90);(Henley: 62); (Joseph: 11, 40, 46, 50-52, 54, 58, 60-61, 64); (Leesburg: 70-73, 116); (Maddox 83, 86); (Milan: 21-22); (Mitchell: 82); (Nelson, Old John: 20); (Orton: 46-49); (Russell: 74, 93-94, 97, 102-103); (Smith: 95); (Stacey: 77); (Terre Haute: 24-25, 41-42); (Wright I: 53); Wright II 108)

Maddox, L. D.: 83, 86

Mays, Dr. Thomas I.: 79

McClarney, Dr. A. J.: 68

McCoy, Dr.: 63

McDonald, James Pinckney Jr.: 89

McDonald, James Pinckney Sr.: 89

McKennzie, B. P.: 60

McMillian, Joseph: 46

McNeeley, Nick: 83

McNeeley, Tommy: 83

Medical Brief: 96

Medicine, National Academy of: 79

Merritt, Mattie: 55

Milan, Ben: 21-22

Milan, Garvin: 22

Miller, Fred: 21

Miller, Jane: 63

Miller, T. S.: 42

Mississippi: (Blue Springs: 63); (Marshall County: 21, 85); (New Albany: 34); (Waterford: 34)

Missouri: (Savannah: 20); (Sedalia: 46)

Mitchell, Dr.: 82

Moore, Walker: 22-23

Moran, Mr.: 37

Morgan, H. P.: 81-82

Morrison, Floria: 50

Morten, Dr. Thomas G.: 79

Moss, Dr. P. B.: 108

Narmore, R. H.: 101

Nashville American, The: 103

Nebraska, Tecumseh: 20

Nelson, Old John: 20

New York: (Buffalo: 21); (New York City: 11, 21, 30, 78); (Staten Island: 78)

North Carolina: 32, 43, 51, 81

Nowles, James: 50

O'Bryan, Carl: 74

O'Bryan, Elmore: 74

O'Bryan, T. C.: 74

Ohio: (Attica: 84); (Columbus: 87); (Delaware County: 87)

Oliver, Fayette: 100

Oliver, Willie: 99

Orton, T. M.: 46-49

Owen, William: 14

Palmore, Fred: 64

Parker, William: 48

Parvin, Dr. Theophilus: 79

Pate, J. B:

Patterson, Mrs. David: 50-51

Patton, T. W.: 50

Pennsylvania, Philadelphia: 19, 21, 78

Pennsylvania, University of: 79

Pierce, Jennie: 96, 101-102

Pirtle, Monte: 23

Press, Giles County: 12

Price, Dr.: 28

Probst, Dr. Charles Oliver: 88

Punty, Ira: 48

Rabies and its Increasing Prevalence: 100

Railroad, Louisville & Nashville: 98

Railroad, Missouri, Kansas & Texas: 46

Randolph, F. P.: 66

Rayburn, W. W.: 98

Reaburn, Dr. J. J.: 49

Redford, W. H.: 108

Reed, Charles: 31

Reneau, Polly: 101

Rice, Clara: 48

Richard the Lionhearted, King: 71

River, Big Harpeth: 37

River, Cedar: 17
River, Stones: 11
Roberts, Dr.: 34
Roberts, Mrs: 77
Roberts, Tom Patterson: 77
Rodes, Robert: 11-12
Rogers, Mrs.: 85
Rogers, Will: 85
Roper, Robert: 67
Rose, Wash: 85
Rose, Mrs.: 85
Russell, J. F.: 74, 93-94, 97, 102-103
Russell, James: 90
Saracen: 71
Scotland: 71
Scott, Sir Walter: 71, 116
Seaton, Mr.: 70
Shearin, George Washington Sr.: 89
Shearin, Raby Bryant: 89
Shelton, Mark: 30
Sheppard, Mr.: 36
Sherrill, Mrs.: 60
Shofner, T. A.: 66
Shofner, Willie: 66
Silcox, Lura Ann: 84-85
Simmons, Solomon: 95
Simpkins, Tom: 53
Small, Dr. Ed: 46
Smiley, Mrs.: 54
Smith, Floy: 66-67
Smith, Irwin: 95

Smith, John: 66
Smith, Mrs. Matt: 67
Snake: (Copperhead: 95); (Rattlesnake: 33); (Water Moccasin, cottonmouth: 44)
Snakestone: 22, 116-117
Society, Aid, Fidelity Mutual Aid: 19
Society, Philadelphia Medical: 79
Society, Upper Cumberland Medical: 68
Spence, Ida: 50
Spenser, D. E.: 53-54
Spider: 22, 95
Stacey, J. B.: 77
State Board of Health, Kansas: 107
State Pasteur Institute, Alabama: 108
Suddath, Link: 98
Sullenger, Penny Ann: 37
Swanner, Mrs.: 28
Tabor, Wheeler Reece: 89
Tabor, William: 89
Talisman, The: 71, 116
Tarantulas: 18
Tennessee: (Adams: 44); (Alamo: 74); (Alexandria: 67); (Bloomington Springs: 68); (Bolivar: 31, 63); (Bunker Hill: 20); (Burt: 77); (Cannon County: 89); (Celina: 84); (Chattanooga: 26, 50); (Cheatham County: 53, 64); (Clay County: 84); (Coffee County: 22-24, 26-28, 35, 73, 89); (Columbia: 40-41, 50, 90); (Crockett County: 74); (Crossville: 52, 68, 89); (Cumberland County:

52); (Davidson County: 19, 53, 60); (Dayton: 50); (Decherd: 55); (DeKalb: 77); (Dickson: 53, 64, 69); (Dickson County: 53); (Dowelltown: 67); (Dresden: 15, 86, 94); (Eagleville: 35); (Edgefield: 11, 38, 40, 50, 54); (Elora: 78); (Estill Springs: 84); (Fairfield: 40, 66); (Fayette County: 25); (Flintville: 28, 36); (Franklin County: 35, 55); (Gallatin: 62); (Gibson County: 102); (Giles County: 11-12, 20); (Grant: 67, 94); (Green Hills: 19); (Hampshire: 50); (Hardeman County: 31); (Hartsville: 98); (Henry County: 14-15, 53, 108); (Henry Station: 15); (Hickman County: 77); (Humboldt: 74, 93, 97); (Humphries County: 53); (Hunter's Point: 26); (Iron City: 40); (Jackson: 62-63); (Kenton: 83); (Kingston Springs: 64); (Knoxville: 104); (Lafayette: 27); (Lawrence County: 102, 107); (Lawrenceburg: 102); (Lebanon: 26); (Leoma: 107); (Liberty: 77); (Lincoln County: 27, 36, 78); (Lynchburg: 30, 35); (Macon County: 27); (Manchester: 60); (Marion County: 82); (Maury City 74, 93, 97); (Maury County: 50, 63); (McEwen: 108); (McMinnville: 70); (McNairy County: 44); (Milan: 83); (Montgomery County: 53, 66); (Moore County: 30); (Nashville: 11, 13-14, 18-19, 32-33, 37-38, 45, 50, 58, 61, 63, 68, 78, 90, 98, 103, 108); (Normandy: 66); (Overton County: 89); (Petersburg: 27); (Pulaski: 11, 20, 27); (Puryear: 108); (Putnam County: 68); (Red Boiling Springs: 69); (Riddleton 61-62); (Ridgetop: 54); (Robertson County: 54); (Rogana: 62); (Rome: 94); (Rutherford: 28, 35); (Shackle Island: 62); (Shelbyville: 13, 15, 35, 60-61, 63, 68, 78, 90, 98, 103, 108); (Shiloh: 62); (Smith County: 61, 67, 94); (Smithville: 22-23); (South Pittsburgh: 82); (Sparta: 74); (Spenser's Mill: 53); (Summitville: 73); (Sumner County; 62); (Trenton: 97); (Trousdale County: 26, 98); (Tullahoma: 60, 73); (Union City: 83); (Wartrace: 66); (Wayne County: 40); (Weakley County: 15); (White County: 70); (Williamson County: 37); (Wilson County: 26); (Woodbury: 67, 89); (Woodland Mills: 83); (Walling: 70)

Texas: (Denton: 62); (Farmersville: 32-33); (Fort Worth: 31); (Mansfield: 32); (Waco: 18)

Treatment, Pasteur: 10, 30, 93, 102-103, 107-108, 110

Trenary, Frank M.: 58-59

Triplet, Mr.: 70

University, Vanderbilt: 98, 103

Vanvalkenburg, G. S.: 45

Vanvalkenburg, William: 45

Vaughn, Henry L.: 108

Vaughn, Mose: 37

Vining, Officer: 38

Virginia: (Alexandria: 72); (Leesburg: 70, 72-73); (Luray: 73); (Lynchburg: 11); (Manchester: 81); (Petersburgh: 99); (Rappahannock County: 72); (Winchester: 71)

Wantland, Henry: 63, 64
Wantland, Samuel N.: 63, 64
Wantland, William: 63, 64
Watson, F. A.: 50
Waugh, Mrs.: 87-88
Webster, Martin: 69
Wetherby, Rodney: 33
Wheeler, Forrest: 37-38
White, Dr. T. E.: 46
White, George: 97
White, Hershel: 97
Whitworth, Sam: 40
Wiggington, Oscar: 40
Wilcox, Dr.: 78
Wilkerson, P. F.: 63
Wilson, Dr.: 27
Winstead, Mr.: 70
Winstead, W. J.: 74
Woods, Dr. Matthew: 79
Woods, Mrs. David: 86
Woodward, Luke E.: 71
Wray, Ike: 74, 94
Wright, Dixie: 108
Wright, Dr. Levin Dickson: 53, 98-99
Zirkle, J. H.: 73

www.ingramcontent.com/pod-product-compliance
Lightning Source LLC
Chambersburg PA
CBHW060810050426
42449CB00008B/1615